"Tom Stuckey boldly stamps with currency older Christian teaching about atonement. He argues that when thinking about God's work of saving human beings we cannot dismiss, as is the wont of some present-day theologians, metaphors such as 'sacrifice' and 'debt.' In a brilliant employment of contemporary culture he shows how these traditional views of divine and human suffering make a decisive difference for the moral life of Christians and non-Christians. All pastors will find this a rich vein for sermon preparation and congregational teaching."

—M. Douglas Meeks
Cal Turner Chancellor Professor of Theology and Wesleyan Studies
Vanderbuilt Divinity School

"Tom Stuckey's book will appeal to theological students and church study groups alike wanting to grapple with the difficult questions of human sinfulness and how God deals with us. He does so using scholarly tools and an acute and lively awareness of the world around us."

—Tim Macquiban
Superintendent Minister
Cambridge Methodist Circuit

The Wrath of God Satisfied?

The Wrath of God Satisfied?

Atonement in an Age of Violence

TOM STUCKEY

WIPF & STOCK · Eugene, Oregon

THE WRATH OF GOD SATISFIED?
Atonement in an Age of Violence

Copyright © 2012 Tom Stuckey. All rights reserved. Except for brief quotations in critical publications or reviews, no part of this book may be reproduced in any manner without prior written permission from the publisher. Write: Permissions, Wipf and Stock Publishers, 199 W. 8th Ave., Suite 3, Eugene, OR 97401.

Wipf & Stock
An Imprint of Wipf and Stock Publishers
199 W. 8th Ave., Suite 3
Eugene, OR 97401
www.wipfandstock.com

ISBN 13: 978-1-62032-050-1
Manufactured in the U.S.A.

All Scripture quotations, unless otherwise indicated, are taken from the Holy Bible, New International Version®, NIV®. Copyright ©1973, 1978, 1984 by Biblica, Inc.™ Used by permission of Zondervan. All rights reserved worldwide.
The Scripture quotations contained herein are from The New Revised Standard Version of the Bible, copyright (c) 1989 by the Division of Christian Education of the National Council of the Churches of Christ in the United States of America, and are used by permission. All rights reserved.

Extracts from the song "In Christ Alone" by Stuart Townsend and Keith Getty. *Admin. by worshiptogether.com songs excl. UK & Europe, admin by Kingswaysongs, a division of David C Cook tym@kinsway.co.uk (Licence PT36-7936) Used by permission. Copyright (c) 2002 Thankyou Music (PRS) (admin. worldside at EMICMGPublishing.com Europe which is adm. By Kingswaysongs) (License No. 525860) All rights reserved. Used by permission.

to Christine

Contents

Preface ix
Abbreviations xiii

PROLOGUE   ATONEMENT TODAY AND YESTERDAY

    1   On the Cross as Jesus Died   3

PART ONE   LIFTING THE CROWN JEWELS

    2   The Battle Won   15

    3   From the Foundation of the World   26

    4   Dishonourable Dealings   35

    5   Love Moved Him to Die   45

    6   Too Much Blood   55

    7   Penal Problems   65

PART TWO   WRATH SATISFIED?

    8   A Wheel of Fire   77

    9   There Is No God   87

    10   Wrath Satisfied   97

    11   Full Atonement Made   107

EPILOGUE   ATONEMENT TODAY AND TOMORROW

    12   Outside a City Wall   119

SERMON   TREES OF TRAGEDY AND TRIUMPH
            "He went and hanged himself." (Matt 27:5)   129

Bibliography   133

Preface

I FIRST STARTED THINKING about the wrath of God fifty years ago when I read C. H.Dodd's exposition of Romans 1:16.[1] I felt he had missed something but was not sure what it was. In 1968 I attended a series of lectures at New College, Edinburgh, on aspects of redemption given by Professor T. F. Torrance. These stimulated a lifelong interest in atonement theology.

More recently I have been asked by Methodist ministers if I could sing all the words of Stuart Townsend and Keith Getty's popular hymn "In Christ Alone,"[2] and questioned about the sentence "the wrath of God is satisfied." When I wrote an article about this I received a lot of perplexing letters—some of them hostile.[3]

My belief in God as mysterious and holy love has sustained me over the years. From my readings of Karl Barth's *Church Dogmatics*, I have increasingly come to appreciate the doctrine of the Trinity—but Trinity understood in a more dynamic way than Barth.

God as Trinity was the theological starting point for my book on mission in an age of violence,[4] while my last book was an attempt to get congregations to think theologically.[5] In 2005 I was appointed President of the Conference of the Methodist Church in Britain. This enabled me to extend my preaching and teaching ministry beyond the United Kingdom. Inspired by the vision of Ezekiel 37, I challenged congregations with the question, "What is the Spirit saying to the churches?" The core of my answer was as follows:

> God is calling us to radical change. He is speaking to us about repentance and conversion! God is telling us to create fresh

---

1. Dodd, *Romans*, 22–24.
2. Extracts taken from the song "In Christ Alone" by Keith Getty & Stuart Townsend Copyright (c) 2001 Thankyou Music. Used by permission.
3. Stuckey, "Wrath Satisfied."
4. Stuckey, *Far Country*.
5. Stuckey, *Pentecost*.

Preface

expressions of church alongside and within the old since much of the old, in its resistance to change, will not survive. Life only comes to our dry bones through prophecy, that is speaking the Word of the Lord (theology) and through the power of the Spirit (Pentecost). Word and Spirit need each other. When the Word is without the Spirit, the church dries up. When the Spirit is without the Word, the church blows up. When Word and Spirit come together, the church grows up. If we are to come alive, attention must be given to theology and to the work of the Holy Spirit.[6]

The "word" for today, I believe, must be about the cross. I write this book to encourage preachers to know nothing "except Jesus Christ, and him crucified" (1 Cor 2:2). To order to give depth and potency to this message, preachers, teachers, and congregations need to turn again to the rich atonement resources of the church. These are the atonement theories, which I refer to as the "crown jewels" of faith.[7]

This book is written to provide theological resources and inspiration for those who, like myself, wish to preach about the cross of Christ. While some preachers are fully equipped for the task, there are others—maybe just starting out—who have little or no awareness of the traditional atonement theories. I have tried to write for both. Because it is not easy combining depth with accessibility, I am more than grateful to the many people who have helped me.

Over the last three years I have given lectures and led study days on atonement theology. These occasions have been stimulating, provocative, and invaluable. Seldom have I come away from such encounters without some new issue to think about. These challenges have meant that I have had to re-write all the chapters of this book more than once. I am nevertheless extremely grateful to the hundreds of people who have contributed in this way.

Certain individuals need a special mention. I wish to thank the Rev. Michael Townsend and Dr. Natalie Watson, who encouraged me in the early stages of writing, and the Rev. Kenneth Howcroft who has provided sound theological insight and challenged some of my readings of Scripture and theology. I have also been able to "try out" chapters on Rev. Margaret Jones and Rev. John Walker at our meetings together. I am grateful for their comments and encouragement. I wish to thank Rev. Dr. Chris

6. Ibid., 5–6.
7. "Crown Jewels."

Preface

Blake for his suggestion that I include a sermon at the end. Thanks are also due to the Rev. Michael Jackson who has gone painstakingly through all the chapters highlighting errors and confusions so enabling me, in the rewrites, to bring greater clarity to the whole. I am also indebted to the Rev. Dr. Michael Thompson, not only for his Biblical scholarship but also for his practical advice in helping me prepare the manuscript for the publisher. I place on record my thanks to Wipf & Stock for accepting my manuscript and for the editorial expertise guidance and understanding of Christian Amondson. I also wish to thank Tina Campbell Owens for helping me prepare the text for publication. Thanks are also due to the staff of Sarum College Library, Salisbury.

Above all I wish to thank my wife Christine, who has not only put up with my book and article writing over the years, but because of my struggles with this particular book has re-organized her life so as to give me space and time to write. Your encouragement alone, Christine, has kept me going particularly when I have felt like giving up. This book is especially dedicated to you.

Tom Stuckey
Ash Wednesday, 2012

Abbreviations

CD	Barth, Karl. *Church Dogmatics*. Edited by G. W. Bromiley and T. F. Torrance. 14 vols. Edinburgh: T & T Clark, 1957–75.
CDH	Anselm. *Cur Deus Homo (CDH)*. In *St. Anselm: Basic Writing*. Translated by S. N. Deane. La Salle, IL: Open Court, 1988.
De Incar.	Athanasius, "De Incarnatione Verbe Dei." In *St Athanasius on the Incarnation*. London: Mowbray, 1953.
MHB	Methodist Hymn Book, London: Methodist Publishing House, 1933.
Inst.	Calvin, John. *Institutes of the Christian Religion*. In vol. 20, *The Library of Christian Classics*. London: SCM Press 1961.
ST & LT	Short Text and Long Text of Julian of Norwich, *Revelations of Divine Love*, translated by E. Spearing, Penguin Books, 1998.
WH	Wesley's Hymns, London: Methodist Book Room, 1872.

PROLOGUE

Atonement Today and Yesterday

1

On the Cross as Jesus Died

ON THE CROSS AS JESUS DIED

For one whole week beginning sixth August 2011 Britain experienced an outbreak of rioting, looting, and burning unlike anything seen for a generation. Starting in Tottenham, civil disorder spread across London, to Brixton, Croydon, Clapham, Ealing, Lewisham, Hackney, East Ham, and Barking. The skyline was tinged with smoke as London burnt. The police were initially unable to hold back the tide of rampaging mobs who had taken control of the streets to raid, loot and burn. Graphic pictures of teenagers smashing shops windows, carrying off goods and trashing stores, were beamed across the world. One of the most telling pictures was of an innocent Malaysian student caught up in the riots. Injured and bloody, he was being helped to his feet and then mugged in broad daylight by thugs posing as Good Samaritans. This suggests to the world that Britain is seriously sick.

Only after several nights when police numbers had been reinforced by thousands of others drawn from the provinces were they able to take back control of the streets. By this time, however, similar outbreaks had occurred across the country in Liverpool, Birmingham, Bristol, Manchester, and elsewhere. The Prime Minister cut short his holiday and a week later Parliament was recalled. By the twelfth of August 1,486 arrests had been made. It was not only teenage gangs who had gone on the looting spree but teenagers from the suburbs. Some parents were also involved.

As police raided homes not only did they encounter households of criminals but also shocked parents who had no idea their child had been on the rampage. Jonathan Sacks comments,

> What we have witnessed is a real, deep seated and frightening failure of morality. They were not rebels with or without a cause. They were mostly bored teenagers, setting fire to cars for fun and looting shops for clothes, shoes, electronic gadgets and flat-screen televisions. If that is not an indictment of the consumer society, what is? . . . Civilization just caught a glimpse of its soul. We have just seen ours and it is not pleasant.[1]

VIOLENCE OUTSIDE AND INSIDE THE CHURCH

Martin Bell, a British reporter and independent Member of Parliament, examines recent wars, human disasters, and the clash of arms beyond our borders.[2] He suggests that violence[3] has become an acceptable part of British culture. This may also be true of the United States, which has been described as "an unbearably violent society."[4]

Violence in Britain is being enacted in obvious things like pornography, video games, criminality, drug abuse, slave trafficking, rape, theft, and pillage. Although it has been argued recently that human beings are becoming less violent this conclusion takes little account of structural and institutional violence where insecurity, poverty, disease, and inequality are pervasive.[5] The hurting and harming of people has also become commonplace in families and businesses and is likely to increase in the present economic climate. Violence is also present in the very "caring" institutions supposedly designed to enhance the quality of life. Violence is also found in the church. It is not confined to those publicized incidents of child abuse or bullying, but arises from the "faith conflicts" played out

---

1. Sacks, *Celebrating*, 48.
2. Bell, *Through Gates*, 1–3.
3. Violence has been defined as "any use of force or coercion that involves some kind of hurt or injury" (Sanders, *Atonement and Violence*, 57).
4. Brueggemann, *Babylon*, 29.
5. Bourke reviews Pinker, *Better Angels*.

between individuals who "know that they are right." Violence and religion go together as Richard Dawkins has been telling us for some time.[6]

There are very few chapters in the Old Testament where acts of violence do not occur. Incidents of atrocity, rape, murder, and ethnic cleansing pack the pages. To make matters worse, many of these acts are sanctioned by God. God, moreover, in some cases personally enters history to harden (Exod 10:1), punish (Exod 9:5), destroy (Gen 19:24), and obliterate (Gen 6:7). It is hardly surprising that many Christians abandon the Old Testament in favour of the New and appeal to the teaching of Jesus.

Unfortunately violence is not absent here. Luke tells us how Jesus preaches the kingdom of God "violently" (16:16). It is a troubling phrase,[7] but no more disturbing than Jesus telling us he is the "strong man" who has come to bind Satan and burgle his house to effect a regime change (Mark 3:27). Many of his actions deliberately provoke a hostile response. Crucifixion seems inevitable.

THE VIOLENT METAPHORS OF CHRISTIANITY

The cross is the central icon of Christianity; sometimes empty and sanitized by the resurrection, sometimes unashamedly depicted as an instrument of torture. When people of other faiths see a crucifix they can sometimes react very strongly, as the following story illustrates:

> The location is a church hall and a group of people of many faiths and none were about to discuss the abuse of human rights. As the business began Albert, one of the representatives, raised his hand and said 'could I protest that we are meeting in a room that displays a hideous image of brutality and torture which the people who put it there find edifying'. Everybody looked at the large crucifix. 'I find that disgusting and would prefer it to be removed.'[8]

In many of the hymns Christians sing, there are violent references to blood and wrath. John Humphrys in his book *In God We Doubt* explains

---

6. Dawkins, *God Delusion*, 31.
7. Marshall, *Luke*, 629.
8. The full story is found in Barrow, "The Cross, Salvation and the Politics of Satire," 99.

why he is an agnostic.[9] Unlike Richard Dawkins,[10] Humphrys retains a profound respect for the Christian faith. He has nevertheless abandoned his Christian upbringing because of certain intellectual difficulties like those found in the explanations of why Christ had to die. "There is a green hill"—although nostalgic and evocative—contains a verse about Christ paying the price of sin.[11] This would not be acceptable to Humphrys, neither would the following two hymns with their references to blood, anger and punishment.

> There is a fountain filled with blood.
> Drawn from Immanuel's veins;
> And sinners, plunged beneath that flood,
> Lose all their guilty stains.[12]

> For what you have done
> His blood must atone;
> The Father hath punished for you his dear Son.
> The Lord, in the day
> Of his anger, did lay
> Your sins on the Lamb, and he bore them away.[13]

What should we do with these metaphors and explanations? Bishop John Shelby Spong is quite clear.

> Sometimes the dead wood of the past must be cleared out so that new life has a chance to grow . . . Not every image used to explain Jesus is worthy of survival. The most obvious candidate for dismissal in my mind is also perhaps the oldest of all interpretations of Jesus. I refer to that image of Jesus as 'divine rescuer'.[14]

---

9. Humphrys, *In God We Doubt*.
10. McGrath, *The Dawkins Delusion*.
11. *MHB*, 180.
12. Ibid., 201.
13. WH, 707. This verse from the hymn "All ye that pass by," appearing in one of the 1872 collections of *Wesley's Hymns* was removed when the hymn reappeared in the 1933 *Methodist Hymn Book*.
14. Spong, *Why Christianity Must Change or Die*, 83.

Keith Ward, one time atheist, is less sure. He thinks something important may still be hidden in outdated ideas.[15] David Tacey believes that even outdated metaphors can be "saturated with infinity."[16]

Our context of violence places the metaphors of blood, punishment, and divine anger on the theological agenda. I shall argue that God is not a divine child abuser, a celestial sadist, nor a Shylock deity demanding payment in flesh. Instead God, as mysterious and wonderful love, transforms deadly violence into creative life-giving energy. This book will show that divine anger or wrath is a necessary ingredient for hope in troubled times.

THE SCANDAL OF THE CROSS

The cross has always been a provocative symbol. Green and Baker in their book, *Recovering the Scandal of the Cross*, tell us that Jesus himself had difficulty in persuading his disciples that the cross was good news rather than bad.[17] Two confused disciples are rebuked with the words "Oh how foolish you are, and how slow of heart to believe all that the prophets have declared! Was it not necessary that the Messiah should suffer these things?" (Luke 24:25–26a).

The most disturbing feature of crucifixion for those living in the first century was not the pain but the exposure to shame. Nailing a naked person drenched in bloody sweat and body excretions to a tree in a public place was the ultimate in humiliation.[18] In the male-dominated hierarchical Roman Empire a man's goal was to increase his honour and thereby his status. Shame, the opposite of honour, meant exclusion.[19] The feminist theologian Elizabeth Johnson argues that in such a culture the sight of a women suffering at the hands of men would not shock because women were constantly ill-treated. Women identify with the cross more than men because the cross challenges "the natural rightness of male dominating rule."[20] This raises some interesting reflections on how atonement theories impact differently on men and women.

---

15. Ward, *The Big Questions in Science and Religion*.
16. Tacey, "Fragments," 171.
17. Green and Baker, *Recovering the Scandal of the Cross*, 13.
18. Hengel, *Crucifixion*.
19. Richardson, *Paul for Today*, 39.
20. Thompson, *Crossing the Divide*, 123.

The Wrath of God Satisfied?

For the Greeks it was madness to suggest that a crucified man could be a son of god; "gods" do not suffer! For Jews, speaking of a crucified Messiah was to gabble nonsense. Jewish law made it clear that any person executed and hung on a tree is cursed by God (Deut 21:22–23). Luke's statements in Acts 5:30, 10:39, and 13:29 are therefore all the more remarkable for in each Jesus is described as hanging "on a tree."

The apostle Paul adds insult to injury to the Corinthians by suggesting that the wisdom and power of God are revealed in the lunacy of the cross (1 Cor 1.18–25). He further stretches this to what they perceive as obscenity by saying that God made the Messiah "to be sin" (2 Cor 5:21).

Why does God hide divine transformation behind the hideous form of crucifixion? God chooses to do so not only to upset our feelings but also to attack our minds. The cross is scandalous because it curses proud intelligence and the desire to dominate. Karl Barth in contemplating the alien nature of the cross says,

> We need to pierce the obscurity, to penetrate the alien, threatening and uncomfortable aspect under which the truth draws near to man, if we are really to see it as truth . . . In the first instance, it does not address us; it contradicts us and demands our contradiction . . . The glory . . . is a glory which is concealed in its opposite, in invisibility, in repellent shame . . . we can only turn away in rejection in view of the menace of its form.[21]

Then comes the hammer blow:

> It is as He attests the truth, Himself, in this form, that He unmasks us as liars.[22]

At root, human nature is at war with God. "As a race we are not even stray sheep, or wandering prodigals merely; we are rebels taken with weapons in our hands."[23] In the cross God is holding up a mirror to us. It reflects the dangerous cracks within human nature from which evil emerges, anger is fed and violence explodes (Mark 7:21).

---

21. *CD* 4/3: 377–379.
22. Ibid., 390.
23. Forsyth, *Positive Preaching and the Modern Mind*, 38.

PRECIOUS METAPHORS

This book is written in the belief that even the less savory metaphors associated with the cross are not rubble to be discarded but precious gemstones which, when touched by the Holy Spirit, illuminate and communicate the reality and efficacy of the death and resurrection of Jesus Christ. In worship these flickering facets drip-feed us with the mystery of God. While the creed simply intones—"Christ died for our sins"; the Eucharistic liturgy positively glows with the inexplicable:

> Who made there a full, perfect, sufficient sacrifice, oblation and satisfaction.[24]

In traditional hymns we sing metaphors of mystery into our souls.

> Paschal Lamb by God appointed, all our sins on Thee were laid;
> By almighty love anointed, Thou hast full atonement made
> All thy people are forgive through the virtue of Thy blood
> Opened is the gate of heaven; peace is made 'twix man and God.[25]

Getty and Townsend's popular hymn "In Christ Alone" is similarly packed with metaphors to illuminate the significance of Christ's death. It also, for some, resuscitates the contentious idea of divine punishment.

> till on that cross as Jesus died,
> the wrath of God was satisfied
> for every sin on him was laid;
> here in the death of Christ I live.
>
> And as he stands in victory,
> sin's curse has lost its grip on me,
> for I am his and he is mine
> bought with the precious blood of Christ.[26]

In these three examples together with the hymns already quoted, we have metaphors of debt, blood, punishment, anger, sacrifice, oblation, satisfaction, God the lamb, substitution, almighty love, forgiveness, access, peace, reconciliation, wrath, victory, curse, communion, purchase,

---

24. *Book of Common Prayer.*
25. *MHB*, 228.
26. Extracts taken from the song "In Christ Alone" by Keith Getty & Stuart Townsend Copyright (c) 2001 Thankyou Music. Used by permission.

and the word "atonement." To treat most of these metaphors as "dead wood" chops away at the mystery of who God is and what he does.

P. T. Forsyth, writing in 1908 against the theological dumbing-down of his own time said, "To throw beliefs overboard, like superfluous cargo, is only too easy . . . We must first know them, then appreciate them. A modern theology must be an appreciation of the old, done lovingly and sympathetically, and with scientific continuity."[27] He argues that the rediscovery of atonement is central to the recovery of spiritual authority, power, and holiness. "To banish the atonement from the creative centre of Christianity is in the long-run so to attenuate Christ as to dismiss him from Christianity."[28]

THE CROWN JEWELS

Explanations of why Jesus had to die have traditionally been labeled "theories of atonement." The phrase "at one" has been in the English language since the fourteenth century. It describes harmony and friendship. William Tyndale made use of the word as a noun when in 1526 he translated the Bible into English. He pondered the Hebrew word "*kippér*" meaning "covering" and coined "at" and "onement."[29] Interpreting its meaning in the New Testament was difficult because Paul uses the Greek word "*hilastérion*" for the Hebrew *kippér* (Rom 3:25). *Hilastérion* can be translated "expiation," "propitiation," or "place of atonement." Putting it crudely and simplistically; expiation is something God does for us; propitiation is something we do to God in order to placate his anger.[30] We shall see in the chapters that follow how divine anger haunts explanations of atonement.

In the Jewel House of the Tower of London you will find the following regal symbols studded with jewels behind bulletproof glass. These are the crown jewels:

1. St Edward's Crown and the Imperial State Crown.

2. The Orb and Scepter.

---

27. Forsyth, *Positive Preaching and the Modern Mind*, 91.
28. Ibid.,128.
29. Sykes, *The Story of Atonement*, 2.
30. McIntyre, *The Shape of Soteriology*, 38.

On the Cross as Jesus Died

3. The Ampoule and Spoon used in the coronation for anointing the monarch.

4. The Swords of State.

The theories of atonement, like the crown jewels, are powerful symbols of coronation and kingdom rule. They are the crown jewels of the church, not trifling trinkets. In part one of this book, I remove them from their dusty vaults to see if they can again enrich and empower the mission of the church. Before proceeding however I make three observations.

First, a comment about the terms I am employing. The word "theory" seems to suggest a comprehensive understanding that tries to "capture" the whole truth. Even though I shall continue to employ the word I nevertheless affirm that we are dealing with a mystery to be explored but never grasped.

Second, I am assuming that each atonement theory has been formulated to address a problem that has arisen in a particular situation. If a church finds itself under siege from forces intent on its destruction, the atonement language will emphasis Christ's victory in battle. If the church is enmeshed in chaos or civil disorder then atonement means the re-establishment of law and order. In a situation of injustice, atonement will demonstrate God's justice. If the church seeks to call its members to costly discipleship then showing Christ's life and death to be an exemplary sacrifice may do the trick. I am assuming that the atonement theories are contextual and utilitarian.[31]

Third, in the atonement treasury of the church you will often find a name attached to each of the crown jewels:

1. The classic theory of "Christ the Victor." Its context is that of battle and warfare—Luther. (chapter 2).

2. The theory of "honor satisfied." Its context is the feudal system—Anselm. (chapter 4).

3. The "moral influence" theory focusing on the love of Christ. Its context is the culture of courtly love—Abelard. (chapter 5).

4. The theory of "penal substitution". Its context is the law-court—Calvin. (chapter 7).

---

31. Moses, *The Sacrifice of God*, 4.

The Wrath of God Satisfied?

This linkage of a name and a theory is of course a simplification.[32] Each theologian, named above, works with several metaphors and often advances more than one explanation of atonement. Their writings are often untidy and seldom systematic. There are also others like Athanasius (chapter 3), Julian of Norwich (chapter 6), René Girard (chapter 8), Augustine and Karl Barth (chapter 10). Although their names are not attached to a particular theory, they bring fresh insight to atonement thinking. We shall encounter these names and theories in the chapters that follow.

Fourth, Britain (following the United States) is now a post-modern, pluralistic, multi-cultural society where, within in any city, there are a multiplicity of contexts, situations, and problems. While there may be some overarching challenges like debt, violence, consumerism, injustice, and secularism, no single atonement theory can adequately address all the problems. To accept diversity is to let multiple voices speak. One overarching explanation, such as penal substitution, will not do. We have to live with theological untidiness and allow atonement theories, old and new, to jostle alongside of each other.

THIS BOOK

Mindful of the cultural gap between the church and the lives of those untouched by the gospel, I begin each chapter with a contemporary story that resonates with an atonement theory. It is no accident that all these stories have violent roots. In the epilogue I consider whether it is possible to identify a theory or theologian who might help us today. Bearing in mind that this book is written for preachers, I conclude with a sermon.

Part one examines each of the crown jewels in turn showing them to be utilitarian and contextual. I also introduce those theological giants of the past associated with the theories. In giving "snapshots" of these persons I allow them speak to us in their own words. Their stories and words will hopefully aid our own explorations of atonement.

Atonement theories, stories and metaphors raise questions about the nature of the God we worship. Chapters 9, 10, and 11 of part two are the creative center of the book. Here I gather up and reflect upon the insights

---

32. I have numbered the crown jewels and the theories. Some may find my correlation of the two helpful, others may not.

PART ONE

Lifting the Crown Jewels

2

The Battle Won

IT WAS BITTERLY COLD on the Waterfront. When yesterday we stood on the top of Table Mountain enjoying the spectacular scenery, Robben Island could be clearly seen. Today, as our small boat thrust out into the bay, mist shrouded everything. We tourists had become travelers in a timeless fog.

What a desolate place this is. Cold and damp we climbed from the boat and ambled over to an abandoned bus. Our little group chatted for a while until a depressive silence descended. Were we thinking of the hundreds of prisoners who had walked up the same slipway as ourselves to be locked up for decades? Finally our driver and guide arrived. The latter had been a prisoner here. He was a cheerful man in his early forties. The engine burst into life and we rattled off bound for the prison complex.

After a tour of the cells our guide took us to a dormitory and stood by one of the beds. It had been his. He told us how as a young teacher he had made a remark about the poor treatment of *bantu* children. In the middle of the night the police raided his home, took him away, accused him of being a Communist—he was a Roman Catholic—and incarcerated him for seven years.

When he had finished telling his story a middle-aged man from our group asked, "How can you bear to return to act as a guide when this place must hold terrible memories?" His answer stunned us.

> Don't you understand? Here I was free. We prisoners were free—not like our guards who were slaves of the system. Because they treated us like dirt they brutalized themselves. They lost their

humanity while we discovered ours! The guards were the prisoners. We were the free men.

A deep silence followed. We had been transformed by his words from tourists seeing sights to pilgrims witnessing liberation. The mist still enshrouded us when we re-embarked, but as we approached Cape Town the sun broke though and blazed with freedom light.

A formidable army of enemies and systems were stacked against the apostle Paul yet he, a prisoner of Jesus Christ, is free. He gives us a shopping list of hardships: multiple attacks, muggings, beatings, imprisonment, torture, shipwrecks, hunger, thirst, nakedness, abandonment, deformation of character, and betrayal (2 Cor 11:23–28). He describes how his chains of captivity had become badges of freedom (Phil 1:12–14). Like our guide on Robben Island, Paul is free and cannot stop telling the freedom story. All demonic rulers, powers, devils, and malevolent structures have been defeated.

> I am convinced that neither death nor life, nor angels, nor rulers, nor things present, nor things to come, nor powers, nor height, nor depth, nor anything else in all creation, will be able to separate us from the love of God in Christ Jesus our Lord (Rom 8:38–39).

DEFEATING THE DRAGONS

Stories describing battles against dragons, devils, and dark forces have always gripped the imaginations of people. They keep resurfacing throughout the ages; appearing today in fantasy literature like J. R. R. Tolkien's *Lord of the Rings* and films like *Star Wars*. Mel Gibson takes up the same theme but gives it a sadomasochistic twist in his film *The Passion of Christ*.

In her essay "Being Delivered from Gibson's Hell," Anne Richards sees his film as a nightmare portrayal of a Jew who enters a holocaust resembling a Bosch painting.[1] She draws our attention to the infernal imagery permeating the film. Satan first appears in sympathetic reasonableness, next as a slithering serpent, snarling parodies of human beings, child demons, and maniacs in Herod's court, sadistic torturers, ugly crowds, and a maggot-ridden corpse. Finally beaten he howls in godless

---

1. Richards, "Being Delivered from Gibson's Hell," 75–80.

The Battle Won

emptiness. Gibson presents Jesus as someone sent to hell with a mission of exorcism.

This concept of a battle against demonic powers goes back to the beginning of time. Some say that the accounts of creation in the Old Testament are drawn from an ancient Babylonian myth in which the watery forces of chaos are personified in the primal dragon—Rahab.[2] Enter hero Marduk. He spreads his net, shoots his arrow, and kills the monster. He cuts the body in two, lifting one half up to form the sky and treading down the other half to form the flat earth, leaving a creative space between. The surrounding waters remain to threaten human existence, as we shall see in the next chapter.

The "Exodus" is another battle story. It tells of Moses' triumph not only over Pharaoh but also over the waters of the Red Sea which bar the way to freedom. Isaiah turns this into a message of hope for the exiles in Babylon.

> Awake, as in the days of old, the generations of long ago! Was it not you who cut Rahab in pieces, who pierced the dragon? Was it not you who dried up the sea, the waters of the great deep; who made the depths of the sea a way for the redeemed to cross over? So the ransomed of the Lord shall return (Isa 51:9–11).

In this Old Testament battle for freedom, Isaiah uses the words "redeemed" and "ransomed" thus making them important ingredients within atonement theology.

In the New Testament we find Jesus—according to Mark—engaged in a violent "invasion-redemption mission."[3] Liberation begins with a dramatic description of the heavens being torn apart (1:10) and ends with the ripping down of the dividing wall of the temple (15:38). Jesus is presented as a "space invader." It is no accident that the name "Jesus" or "Savior" comes from the Hebrew root word for "space" (*yasha*). Following his baptism Jesus invades the wilderness turning it into a Garden of Eden. Then follows a mission to village, town, countryside, sea, and city. At each stopping place he reclaims the space occupied by hostile powers. Demons are driven out, (1:25–34), sin and sickness removed (2:9), the oppressive religion of Scribe and Pharisee undermined (3:1–6). Jesus is plundering the property of the strong man, Beelzebul (3:23–27)—who

---

2. Dillistone, *The Christian Understanding of the Atonement*, 79.
3. Gruenler, "Atonement in the Synoptic Gospels," 99–104.

is the latest manifestation of the dragon. The chaotic waters are tamed (4:39, 6:48) and death is destroyed (5:38–42). Christ comes to give his life as a "ransom for many" (10:45). Mark's message is a prequel of Gibson's sadistic mission of exorcism.

Matthew depicts resurrection as victory in a noisy cosmic battle (28:1–4). In the thunder of an earthquake an angel descends, "His appearance was like lightening and his clothing white as snow." This is no fallen angel like Satan, but a triumphant Michael—a risen Christ avatar. The angel rolls away the stone and, in a closing gesture of defiance, sits upon it. The terror-stricken guards, frozen with fear, become like dead men.[4]

The music of victory over the dragon plays throughout the New Testament. Paul's affirmation in Roman 8 springs from his conviction that Christ has "disarmed the rulers and authorities" and triumphed over them on the cross (Col 2:15). The first chapter of Ephesians is a coronation anthem—vibrant with jewel-like metaphors of atonement—celebrating a Trinitarian God and declaring that all things have been put under Christ's feet. The book of Revelation also majors on the worship of the Trinity and the destruction of the dragon.[5] Ethelbert Stauffer, writing in 1939, argues that the idea of victory dominates the New Testament. "The early Church put these thoughts into an eloquent formula . . . Christ is the 'Victor' who has beaten down the ancient enemy in the battle of his passion."[6]

THE CORONATION OF A KING

Although Christ the "Victor" may indeed be a dominant metaphor in the New Testament it is not the only one. Alongside it is the complementary idea of Christ the "King." Christ's invasion-redemption-mission is the work of a king re-claiming his lost kingdom.[7] As a proof text of Christ's victorious kingship, the New Testament repeatedly uses Psalm 110.[8]

> The Lord says to my lord, 'Sit at my right hand until I make your enemies your footstool.' The Lord sends out from Zion your mighty scepter. Rule in the midst of your foes . . . The Lord is at

4. Mathews-Green, "Rising Victorious," 44.
5. Dillistone, *The Christian Understanding of the Atonement*, 91.
6. Stauffer, *New Testament Theology*, 130.
7. Brunner, *The Mediator*, 552.
8. Goldingay, *Psalms 90–150*, 229.

your right hand; he will shatter kings on the day of his wrath (Ps 110:1–2, 5).

This Psalm could be describing the coronation of David or Solomon. It is quoted in Matt 22:44; Mark 12:36; Luke 20:43 leaving readers in no doubt that Jesus is king (Matt 27:37; Mark 15:26; Luke 23:38). This affirmation is not needed in John's Gospel since Jesus announces his kingship to Pilate (John 18:36). Easter and Pentecost are public manifestations of his kingship. God has made him both Lord and Messiah (Acts 2.32–36). Psalm 110 is embedded in Peter's Pentecost sermon about resurrection, exaltation, and elevation. John has similar references to the lifting up of Christ (3:14, 8:28, 12:32, 12:34). Christ's kingship is universal and cosmic. The crown jewels of atonement decorate Christ's coronation.

Psalm 110 also appears in Hebrews 1:13. This letter comes from the context of temple rather than battlefield. Verse 4 from the above Psalm makes this religious setting explicit. "You are a priest forever according to the order of Melchizedek" (Heb 7:17).

Christ is not only "King" but also "Priest." The writer of Hebrews develops this motif in full. Thus from the New Testament's dominant coronation metaphors of "victor" and "king" come a cascade of gemstones—deliverance, liberation, exodus, ransom, and redemption. And coming from the temple context—priest, sacrifice, offering, and blood. These metaphors will be employed by the church throughout its two thousand year history to bring a sparkling spontaneity to the message of cross and resurrection.

AFTER THE NEW TESTAMENT

The church of the second century was constantly under attack so attention inevitably focused on the "victor" theme. Outbreaks of persecution, often state sponsored, were frequent. At the same time a wide range of new philosophical ideas were subverting the Christian message.

Irenaeus, Bishop of Lyon (130–202), came to office following the martyrdom of his predecessor. He had to defend the church against political attacks and hostile philosophical speculations. He himself would be killed in an outbreak of violence. In his book *Against Heresies* he affirms the apostolic tradition and reworks the Pauline motif of Christ "the new Adam" (Rom 5:14; 1 Cor 15:22). The first man had bequeathed a legacy of

The Wrath of God Satisfied?

sin through his disobedience. Christ reverses the fall through his obedience. Irenaeus interprets the reference to the "gathering up of all things in Christ" (*anakephalaiōsis*) (Eph 1:10) as a "recapitulation."

> For as the Lord was man in order to be tested, so also he was Word in order to be glorified . . . and he recapitulated in himself the work originally fashioned.[9]

This atonement insight was encapsulated by John Henry Newman:

> O loving wisdom of our God!
> When all was sin and shame,
> A second Adam to the fight
> And to the rescue came.[10]

Irenaeus said the dragon was a liar who captured Adam and Eve through deception.[11] Gregory of Nyssa—writing two centuries later—argued it was therefore legitimate for God to use trickery since the devil used lies. God goes on a fishing trip. Jesus is the bait. The devil, blinded by his lust for power, sees only the vulnerable humanity of God's Son. He takes a bite. Gulps him down. Gets hooked on the hidden divinity, and is "taken out."[12] Like the Greek Trojan-Horse it is an imaginative strategy for defeating an enemy.

Not all agreed that this was a proper way for God to act. Origen of Alexandria (185–254), believing Satan to be one of God's creatures and not a rival God, pressed for "devil's rights" and insisted that he be treated fairly and paid a ransom.

We have already come across "ransom" in Mark 10:45. Although the word *lutron* indicates "deliverance" it does not exclude the idea of a payment. Mark's mention of "servant" in the same passage reminds us of Isaiah 53:10, "you make his life an offering for sin." But to whom should the ransom be paid? This question was not easily answered and continued to prompt discussion throughout the following centuries.

When Christianity became the state religion following Constantine's famous victory at the Milvian Bridge (AD 312), the conquering 'victor' theme began to fade in the Western Church. Some said it was because

---

9. *Against Heresies*, 127–135.
10. *MHB*, 74.
11. Athanasius, *Against Heresies*, 173.
12. Aulen, *Christus Victor*, 103.

The Battle Won

the church was no longer fighting a hostile State.[13] Certainly many Christians became comfortable, though this was not true of the monks and hermits who in their pursuit of holiness withdrew to the desert to fight against the flesh and the devil. When the Roman Empire started to fall apart in the fifth century it seemed to the peoples of France, Italy, and Spain that the rampaging powers of darkness had again been released.[14] In the harsh centuries that followed, human existence was reduced to a daily battle against fear, hostile attack, disease, hunger, sudden death, and evil spirits. It was a fight that was often lost. Was Christ still king? Whale, in his book, identifies three metaphors—all of them taken from situations of violence—Christ as "Victor," Christ as "Victim," and Christ as "Criminal."[15] In those dark times people were drawn to representations of Christ as the "sacrificial victim" or as the "criminal" paying a penalty to the Judge of all the earth.

The Last Judgment hung like a poisonous cloud over Europe's inhabitants. The church alone, like Noah's Ark, was believed to be the only place of refuge. Through its sacraments and the merits of the saints people could be saved. All this was to change in the sixteenth century when the secular winds of worldliness began to blow across Europe.[16]

AN EXPLOSION OF GRACE

Martin Luther's discovery of a gracious God created a nuclear explosion of heat and light, blasting a hole in church and society from which it has still not recovered. He re-energized the battlefield metaphor. His first fight was internal as he, like many before him, tried to escape the wrath of God.

> A man sees nothing but hell; no escape is before his eyes . . . for it is not the wrath of a mortal man, which has a limit, but the wrath of the eternal God which can never have an end.[17]

Luther had valiantly participated in all the sacramental processes prescribed by the church but had found no relief. His internal struggle

---

13. Boersma, *Violence, Hospitality, and the Cross*, 155.
14. Chadwick, *History of Christianity*, 41.
15. Whale, *Victor and Victim*, 360.
16. De Bourchgrave, *A Journey Into Christian Art*, 45.
17. Rupp, *The Righteousness of God*, 107.

The Wrath of God Satisfied?

was only resolved when he began to lecture on the Psalms and the letters of Paul. God, he discovered, was not against him but for him (Rom 8:31). Christ has exchanged our defeat for his victory.

> Because he had taken upon him our sins, not by constraint, but of this own good will, it behoved him to bear the punishment and wrath of God not for his own person but for our person. So making a happy change with us . . . and gave unto us his innocent and victorious person.[18]

Provoked by the hard sell of indulgences, Luther pressed for a public debate. His internal fight immediately becomes external when the newly invented printing press flooded Christendom with thousands of copies of the *ninety-five theses* he had nailed to the doors of the church in Wittenberg. The fuse for an explosion had been lit.[19]

When the German princes in 1529 formally protested against Rome's attempt to limit the freedom of "the Word," Luther wrote his famous Reformation hymn.[20] It is impregnated with battle imagery and takes up Mark's reference (3:27) to a "stronger man".

> With force of arms we nothing can,
> Full soon were we down-ridden;
> But for us fights the proper Man,
> Whom God himself hath bidden.[21]

Other Reformation hymns reflect Luther's conviction that Christ is "Victor".

> It was a strange and dreadful strife,
> When Life and Death contended;
> The victory remained with Life,
> The reign of Death is ended;
> Striped of power, no more he reigns;
> An empty form alone remains;
> His sting is lost for ever.[22]

---

18. Luther, *Galatians*, 275.
19. Chadwick, *History of Christianity*, 203.
20. Atkinson, *Martin Luther and the Birth of Protestantism*, 280.
21. *MHB*, 494.
22. Ibid., 210.

The Battle Won

In his commentary on Galatians, Luther's words remind us of Paul's statement in Romans quoted near the start of this chapter:

> Through Christ we are made free from the wrath of God, law, sin, death, the power of the devil, hell etc . . . for Christ hath made me free and delivered me from them all. Likewise death, which is the most mighty and most dreadful thing in the whole world is utterly vanquished.[23]

Like Paul, Luther has his own list of tyrants. Chief amongst them were sin, death, the devil, the law and the wrath of God.[24] These tyrants, for Luther, had a personal presence. Christ's victory, however, not only strips them of their supernatural personalities but also empties them of their power to harm.

CHRISTUS VICTOR—THE ANSWER?

Scholars have questioned whether Christ's victory over the dark powers is the primary motif of atonement theology.[25] Gustaf Aulen—who was Professor of Systematic Theology in the University of Lund—believed it was. His 1931 book entitled *Christus Victor* argued that the "classical theory" of Christ "the Victor" planted in the Eastern Church by Irenaeus and resurrected by Luther for the Western Church should take priority over all other theories.[26] Aulen (like Stauffer above), writing in the brooding years before the onslaught of the Nazi terror has allowed his context to shape his conclusion. This is not to say he was wrong but rather to recognize the dynamic relationship between context and message.

This atonement theory is not without its difficulties. First, battlefield imagery is violent. One of the recurring criticisms of atonement theories is the way in which they involve God in acts of violence.

Second, for Luther the tyrants, possibly with the exception of sin, seem to press in upon humanity violating personal space and crushing the human spirit. The theory fails to deal adequately with the wickedness that can spring up inside a person—something Charles Wesley calls "inbred sin." Moreover this evil not only lodges within individuals but acquires a

23. Luther, *Galatians*, 442–443.
24. Watson, *Let God be God*, 124–125.
25. Lohse, *Martin Luther's Theology*, 227.
26. Aulen, *Christus Victor*, 109.

corporate reality through destructive community myths, memories, and stories. Even though we may be liberated from our external chains, a slave mentality can endure. One-time victims in an exuberance of freedom often go on to become the oppressors of the next generation. Just think about Robert Mugabe!

Third, we delude ourselves if we think evil is defeated. Aulen anticipates victory over Hitler, yet no sooner is that war over than the Cold War begins. The dragon moves from Vietnam, to Cambodia, the countries of Africa, back to the Balkans, on to Iraq, Afghanistan, Somalia, Iran, and Syria. The dragon although defeated does not accept defeat and keeps transposing himself. Evil remains—pervasive and intractable. Christ has overcome it but has not yet obliterated it.

AN AGENDA OF LIBERATION

Explaining atonement in terms of freedom and liberation from external powers does make it readily applicable in many contexts since every age and place is subject to its own oppressive tyrants.

Liberation theology is a twentieth-century re-working of "Christus Victor." Priests and ministers working amongst the poor in Latin America had come to see that the debilitating effects of poverty could only be removed by challenging the tyrannical powers that had infiltrated the political and economic structures under which they lived. Their action, like that of Jesus was to engage in an "invasion-redemption-mission" to secure a new Exodus for the oppressed.[27] In South Africa, "liberation" was a key metaphor used in the struggle against Apartheid.[28] Thus we find ourselves returning to where this chapter began; to South Africa, Apartheid, and Robben Island.

Our guide on Robben Island spoke of incarceration and freedom. Paul writing to the Philippians from his prison cell said much the same. Luther, who also knew imprisonment, similarly encourages the persecuted Christians of Miltenberg.

> Be glad and thank God that you have been counted worthy to hear and learn his Word and suffer for it . . . Pity your enemies because . . . they have only the sad and wretched consolation of

---

27. Boff, *Jesus Christ Liberator*.
28. De Gruchy, *Reconciliation*, 65.

the devil . . . This is a joyful victory and conquest, won without sword and fist . . . If we live, they will not have peace in our presence. If we die, they will have peace even less . . . In a word they will not be rid of us . . . This is my prophecy, and it will not fail. May God in his grace and mercy keep you, dear friends.[29]

---

29. Luther, *Letters of Spiritual Counsel*, 202, 207.

3

From the Foundation of the World

ON THE TWENTIETH OF April 2010 there was an explosion on a Transocean deepwater drilling rig forty-two miles off the coast of Louisiana in the Gulf of Mexico. Eleven workers were killed. The rig sank and oil gushed out. This particular rig was tapping oil in 5,000 feet of water and a further 13,000 feet beneath the seabed. Efforts to activate the shut-off valve were unsuccessful.

As distressed oil-covered pelicans began to be seen on the beaches around New Orleans the President pledged his help. The British Petroleum (BP) Chief Executive Tony Hayward said the company would take full responsibility for containment, the cost of the clean up and legitimate claims for compensation. By the beginning of May the sheer scale of the disaster was becoming apparent. All of BP's attempts to plug the leak failed. By now the oil spill covered thousands of square miles of sea. The executives of BP and the other companies involved appeared before a congressional hearing blaming each other. On the nineteenth of May the first heavy oil hit the fragile Louisiana marshlands and another slick entered a powerful current able to carry it to Florida Keys. BP shares plunged. The exasperated authorities placed fishing restrictions covering 37 percent of US federal waters in the Gulf. It was estimated that up to 1.7 million gallons of oil had flowed out; an estimate far higher than that quoted by BP. Further criticism of BP came from a part owner of the well, who described BP's behavior as so "reckless" as to verge on "gross neglect." On the twenty-seventh of June, oil washed ashore in mainland Mississippi.

From the Foundation of the World

In our last chapter we focused on victory over the dragon who inhabits systems and structures which oppress and crush. In this chapter we explore how these same powers of destruction ravage the planet. We have already seen how the earth, in the ancient myths, was believed to be the product of a primal cosmic battle. The Hebrews believed the earth to be supported on two pillars: a pillar of justice and a pillar of righteousness (Ps 97:2).[1] If a crack appeared in either, the ecological system would become unbalanced (Ps 82). If a serious rupture occurred, then the primal waters would burst in destroying all life—which is what happened in the flood (Gen 7:11).

The Western world's obsession with oil and the technological drive for power is resulting in the rape, exploitation, and pollution of our natural environment. James Lovelock's disturbing book *The Revenge of Gaia*,[2] tells us we can no longer treat the earth as an inanimate object. We are in a symbiotic relationship with a living organism so that "if we fail to take care of the earth, the earth will surely take care of itself by making us no longer welcome." Atonement theory must therefore say something about the earth that sustains us. In our last chapter Jesus as victor invaded time and space to fight the powers of the dragon. In this chapter we focus on Jesus the Son of God at work with the Father before time and space began.

DRIVEN FROM PARADISE

The traditional doctrine of the fall begins with the story of Adam and Eve. It describes how through disobedience sin enters the world. Ceasing to be priests of creation the primal pair bequeath a bitter legacy. The partnership between male and female collapses into patriarchy. The gentle relationship between human beings and the earth is brutalized. Women, like the ground itself, are exploited and raped. Such was the escalation of violence that the spiritual boundary between the heaven and earth was violated (Gen 6). The pillars of justice and righteousness cracked and the primal waters of chaos poured in to flood the earth.

Overcome with grief (Gen 6:6), God in a lifeboat operation gives humanity a second chance. His first act of creation was a sabbatical celebration. In this second act of repopulation we see God's resignation. He

---

1. Fox, *Original Blessing*, 184.
2. Lovelock, *Revenge of Gaia*, 2–3.

sadly realizes that man's mind has become warped. The divine charge to humankind in this post-diluvium era has a bitter meaning as he anticipates the unfolding of a "decreation" story reversing the very aims he first had in mind (Gen 9:2–3). The planet's story becomes shrouded in such bleakness that the eighth century prophet Isaiah exclaims,

> The earth shall be utterly laid waste and utterly despoiled; for the Lord has spoken this word. The earth dries up and withers ... The earth lies polluted under its inhabitants; for they have transgressed laws, violated statutes, broken the everlasting covenant. Therefore a curse devours the earth and its inhabitants suffer for their guilt (Isa 24:3–6a).

Alongside one of Isaiah's grim passages, there is also a planetary message of hope.

> The wilderness and the dry land shall be glad the desert shall rejoice and blossom; like the crocus ... Then the eyes of the blind will be opened and the ears of the deaf unstopped ... For waters shall break forth in the wilderness and streams in the desert (Isa 35).

Although Israel has forsaken God's covenant, God remembers it and like a woman in childbirth promises to deliver a new creation (Isa 42:14b–16). Paul uses a similar feminine analogy of hope when describing creation "groaning" in labor pains (Rom 8:22).

FROM THE FOUNDATION OF THE WORLD

The opening stanzas of John's Gospel speak of Christ "the Word" (*logos*) being with the Father and involved in the act of creating (1:1). Moreover, Christ "the Word" is not only the sacrificial "Lamb of God" who takes away the sin of the world (1:29), he is the "Lamb of God" slain from the foundation of the world (Rev13:8).

This cosmic perspective is found in the opening chapter of Ephesians where a theology of election and predestination presents Christ both as the center of history and as the author of that history. This entire passage builds on the Colossian description of a cosmic Christ through whom, by whom and for whom "all things have been created" (Col 1:16). Ephesians, like John's Gospel, anchors hope beyond the vagaries of history. Hope for humanity and the planet have been rooted in Christ from the very beginning (John 1:3–4).

To illuminate this hope the writer of Ephesians uses the word, *oikonomia* (Eph 1:10, 3:2, 3:9).[3] It is related to the Greek word for "house" (*oikos*). From this we get terms like "ecumenical" and "economics." It is about "housekeeping." The writer of Ephesians likens humanity to a dysfunctional family indulging in bad housekeeping. To put it another way, the world's economy is failing because gross selfishness and mutual exploitation have made the ecological systems operating on and within our planet unsafe. The author's vision is of an alternative household where God does the housekeeping. The writer suggests that God's new organism, the body of Christ, will expand and grow permeating and transforming the failed systems of this world. This vision would have been lost had it not been for Athanasius (296–373) who championed the Apostolic Faith and defended the divine *Logos* against those who did not realize that the very basis of God's planetary program of restoration was at stake. If Christ was not involved with the Father in the first act of creation then how could his death and resurrection issue in a new creation?

ATHANASIUS AGAINST ALL COMERS

The context of battle is no longer the martyrs' arena but the University of Alexandria. The metaphor of "Christ the Victor" remains central but the fight is now over the words used to explain this.

Athanasius was born in Alexandria and grew up in the turbulent years of terror which final ended with Constantine's victory (AD 312). Athanasius may have witnessed the killing of some of his friends. He would certainly know of others who had sought refuge in the Egyptian desert. The latter would never return to city life because in wilderness solitude they discovered a renewing form of ascetic piety which was to blossom into monasticism.

Unfortunately the ending of persecution did not mark the termination of trouble for the church. Intoxicating intellectual ideas like an unstoppable oil spill surged up to pollute the seas of "Apostolic Faith." The chief proponent of this dangerous thinking was an Alexandrian presbyter called Arius.

---

3. Lincoln, *Ephesians*, 32–35, 173.

> God was not always a father . . . only later did he become a father. The Son did not always exist . . . The *Logos* of God came into existence out of nothing . . . There was a time when he was not.[4]

Arius was deposed by the patriarch but would not accept his ruling. He sought allies from elsewhere. These were easily found given the cultural tensions and jealousies that existed between Alexandria and the other major centers of Christendom. In 325, Athanasius attended the Council of Nicea where he drafted the phrase *homoousion* (the same substance) to make it crystal clear that Jesus Christ was not created by the Father but had forever shared divinity with the Father.

The church has always been tempted in the interests of mission to simplify or dumb-down complicated theological notions. The teaching of Arius was captivating because it was easy to understand and resonated with the spirituality of the time. Athanasius realized that the teaching of Arius was subversive because it robbed the Gospel of the fullness of salvation. It reduced the work of Christ to the saving of souls rather than the recreation of the whole human person, mind, body, and soul and ignored the restoration of God's creation.

DE INCARNATIONE

The theological basis for Athanasius' life-long advocacy of the *homoousion* had been set out in a small book entitled *On the Incarnation* (*De Incarnatione*) written in 318 when still a young cleric in the Patriarch's household. He argues that all of the Greek gods are fading away because Christ has completely banished fear, savage habits, and brutality.

> By his Godhead (he has) confounded and overshadowed the opinions of the poets and the delusions of the daemons and the wisdom of the Greeks, it must be manifest and will be owned by all that He is in truth Son of God, Existent Word and Wisdom and Power of the Father.[5]

Such is Athanasius' stress on the Godhead of Christ that he is in danger of allowing Christ to usurp the initiatives of the Father.

---

4. McGrath, *Christian Theology*, 333.
5. *De Incar.* 54, 87.

> He saw how unseemly it was that the very things of which He Himself was the Artificer should be disappearing. He saw how the surpassing wickedness of men was mounting against them. He saw also their universal liability to death. All this He saw and, pitying our race, moved with compassion for our limitation . . . He took to Himself a body, a human body even as our own . . . He the Mighty One, the Artificer of all, Himself prepared this body in a virgin as a temple to Himself.[6]

His enemies thought Athanasius was actually replacing the human mind and soul with the divine *logos* so making Christ other than truly human. Athanasius nevertheless presses his argument:

> His body was for Him not a limitation, but an instrument, so that He was both in it and in all things, and outside of all things, resting in the Father alone. At one and the same time—this is the wonder—as Man He was a living human life, and as Word He was sustaining the life of the universe, and as Son He was in constant union with the Father.[7]

Athanasius defends his "high" Christology because he sees no inconsistency between God's act of creation and God's act of salvation.[8] The fall of Adam marks a pivotal moment when creation moves from a state of immortality to mortality[9] so that the divine image in humanity is defaced and everything falls into corruption. God, the *Logos,* who shared in the original act of creation, reverses Adam's fall and thereby renews the divine image in humanity.

> Who save the Word of God Himself, Who also in the beginning made all things out of nothing . . . His part it was and His alone both to bring again corruption to incorruption and to maintain for the Father His consistency of character with all.[10]

The Word, by dwelling in a human body, initiates an unstoppable process of divinization. The resurrection of Christ's body is a foretaste of the divinization of all flesh as God "makes us all divine."[11] Athanasius ex-

---

6. *De Incar.* 8, 34.
7. *De Incar.* 17, 45.
8. *De Incar.* 1, 26.
9. Schmiechen, *Saving Power*, 172.
10. *De Incar.* 7.
11. *MHB,* 142.

pounds the optimism of grace found in Ephesians where Christ, as head of the church, fills all with the "measure of all the fullness of God" (Eph 3:19).

> The Word of God thus acted consistently in assuming a body and using a human instrument to vitalize the body. He was consistent in working through man to reveal Himself everywhere, as well as through the other parts of His creation, so that nothing was left void of His Divinity and knowledge.[12]

TRANSCENDENCE AND IMMANENCE

There is a problem. All the protagonists in the Arian controversy used metaphysical terms (like *homoousion & homoiousion*) to describe divinity.[13] Such terminology is now considered to be static and impersonal. Moreover, the word *logos* is associated with male objectivity and rationality. Whenever, in the works of the Church Fathers, the male *logos* inhabits flesh, the body is regarded as an instrument or object.

Sallie McFague in her book *The Body of God* reacts against this machine model of the physical world. She concludes: "to see the world differently, not anthropocentrically, not in a utilitarian way, not in terms of dualistic hierarchies, not in parochial terms. We need a sense of belonging to the earth, of having a place in it, and of loving it more than we ever thought possible."[14]

---

12. *De Incar.* 45.

13. The Council of Nicea did not end the theological battle because the anti-Alexandrian faction persuaded Emperor Constantine to reinstate Arius. Arius and his supporter realized that the *homoousion* and Athanasius, who had now become bishop following the sudden death of the patriarch, stood in their way. They launched a full-scale verbal attack accusing him of bribery, extortion and murder. (Anatolios, *Athanasis*, 86–89.) Even the new Emperor Constantius was caught in their intrigue. Athanasius fled into the Egyptian desert seeking refuge amongst the monks. His enemies now pressed their case against the *homoousion* suggesting other words, for example *homoiousion* (of like substance). Athanasius fought on making defensive theological forays from the desert. The Arian controversy raged for fifty years outliving Athanasius and his first protagonists. "Never was so much energy", says Gibbons, "spent on a single vowel." (McGrath, *Christian Theology* 335.) Finally in AD 381 the *homoousion* was triumphant and became the benchmark of all later Trinitarian doctrine.

14. McFague, *The Body of God*, 111.

From the Foundation of the World

She uses the technical terms "transcendence," and "immanence." The former lays stress on God existing apart from his creation while immanence emphasises God's existence and presence within creation. She argues that the incarnation is not about God visiting our world as a tourist. God is not outside the physical world but within it. "His/her transcendence is embodied."[15] God is "the pre-eminent or primary spirit of the universe... we speak of her as the inspired body of the entire universe."[16] McFague's understanding is not dissimilar from James Lovelock (mentioned at the beginning of this chapter). His "Gaia" is McFague's "embodied God" but with a difference; her description is not as mechanistic. Unfortunately McFague goes too far. In lodging God's transcendence totally within creation she reduces transcendence to immanence. Athanasius is important to this discussion because he refuses to sacrifice the one for the other but rather demonstrates the "convergence of divine transcendence and immanence."[17] In so doing he preserves the "otherness" of God, demonstrates how physical existence has been impregnated with hope, and shows how human corruption can be transformed into glory.

A NEW CREATION STORY

McFague wishes for a new creation story to supplant the traditional description of the fall. Clare Amos obliges by suggesting that the Eden story is not so much about "fall" as about education.[18] She asks, cannot Genesis 3 be read as a story of the maturing of human beings? Isn't our quest for knowledge and our desire to make our own decisions a characteristic of children growing towards autonomy and learning to be independent of their parents? Adam and Eve acquire knowledge and come of age freed from dependence on a parental divinity. Of course there are consequences as we get older and learn of our mortality. A shadow dimension gets woven into the process of human growth and evolution.

When such hope is rooted in Christ before the foundation of the world we have grounds for optimism. In Mark, Matthew, and Luke; crucifixion, resurrection, ascension, and Pentecost are strung-out in time. In

15. Ibid., 133.
16. Ibid., 20.
17. Anatolios, *Athanasius*, 205.
18. Amos, *Beginning Over Again*, 12–19.

The Wrath of God Satisfied?

John, these events are encapsulated in a single moment. Jesus is lifted up on the cross, he is raised up in resurrection, and he breathes Spirit into his disciples (John 20:22). But there is a further dimension of divine infusion.

> He has let himself be overcome by death so that death would gulp him down into the innermost depths of the world. In this way, having descended to the very womb of the earth . . . he could give the earth his divine life forever.[19]

Jesus not only gatecrashes hell, he plants seeds of hope in physical things. The garden of tomb and resurrection are one of the same. The cross is the new tree of life. The meeting between Mary and Jesus parallels the conversation between Adam and Eve—but with an entirely different outcome. The Garden of Eden story is reversed (John19:41). The journey is from Apocalypse to Genesis.[20]

In the Sistine Chapel in Rome, there are two visual representations of the future. Over the altar is Michelangelo's terrifying painting of the last judgment. On the ceiling are nine panels depicting the Genesis story from God the creator to the drunkenness of Noah. It was a moment of illumination when I learnt that Michelangelo Buonarotti did not begin by painting God and then move through the stages of creation to the deluge. He started with Noah's drunkenness and worked backwards, thus reversing the de-creation story.

We saw in the last chapter that "Christus Victor" failed to address "inbred sin." Similarly, the optimistic vision of this chapter with its emphasis on the restoration of the divine image does not take account of the flawed fatalities of the human mind and will. Violence and chaos continue to take on powers of their own and can surge up suddenly from the deep like a polluting oil spill. The divine image, like a flickering candle, can be extinguished when the hurricanes of evil howl. The deification vision of Athanasius disappeared in the Western Church with the collapse of the Roman Empire. Survival would henceforth be the-name-of-the-game, as violence, barbarism, brutality, and chaos flooded the earth. Hope for humanity did endure—but only just! We shall see in our next chapter how a different kind of atonement theory made this possible.

---

19. O'Leary, "Caught between earth and heaven."
20. Primavessi, *From Apocalypse to Genesis*.

4

Dishonorable Dealings

When, in 2009, the *Daily Telegraph* in London began to publish the dark secrets of the expenses of Members of Parliament (MPs), the British electorate was shocked. Initially those MPs with questionable claims hid behind the rules and were unwilling to admit they had done anything wrong. Although named they refused to be shamed.

Some months before there had been a public outcry against the extravagant bonuses awarded to certain top bankers whose recklessness had plunged the nation into debt. People were asking how Sir Fred Goodwin could walk away with a £16.9 million pay off. Why, asked others, should Peter Cummings the former head of corporate banking at HBOS take a £1.12 million pension top-up? Have they no shame?[1]

Each day as new revelations of the Members' expenses appeared, public anger grew. We read how the taxpayers' money was being used to clear mortgages, pay for hedge-trimming, moat clearing, massage chairs, and pornographic videos. We learnt about "flipping"—the practice of claiming expenses for one home while living in another.

> "They are milking the system."
> "They are in it for all they can get."
> "I shall never trust a politician again."
> "These people are unfit to hold office."
> "The honorable members have behaved dishonorably."

---

1. Fred Goodwin has since been stripped of his knighthood.

These were just a few of the comments expressed by a disgusted public. It was as if the surface pomp and splendor of the "Mother of Parliaments" had been ripped off to expose shabby politicians in a self-serving-system.

THE DISAPPEARANCE AND RE-APPEARANCE OF HONOR

By the second half of the last century, the virtue of "honor" as "high respect, good reputation, and nobleness of mind" was fading.[2] Traditional hierarchical elements in society were crumbling. Rank, exalted position, and family name ceased to carry weight. The ethical opposite of "honor" is "shame." The antics of the politicians in the House of Commons and similar shenanigans in the House of Lords may be putting honor back on the public agenda. Similarly the outrageous bonuses given to bankers have resuscitated the cry of "shame."

Honor is important in other societies and cultures. The Prophet Muhammad had said, "Truly your blood, your property, and your honor are inviolable."[3] Terrorists, unfortunately, pursue vengeance as a matter of *Izz'at* (honor). Even though Islam does not condone "honor-related crimes" many "honor killings" take place in Britain every year.

Of the atonement theories, the name of Anselm is linked with "honor." Christ dies to satisfy God's honor. This sound-bite is not only considered to be the sum total of what Anselm said but the word "satisfy" has become associated with unpalatable understandings of the cross.[4] If the virtue of honor is making a comeback in Britain then maybe Anselm still has something important to say.

WHO WAS ANSELM?

He was born in North Italy in 1033. After some undisciplined early years he settled down to became a scholar at the Benedictine Monastery of Bec under the directorship of a fellow-countryman, Lanfranc. Anselm, finding what he had been looking for, took monastic vows. His remarkable

2. *The Oxford Dictionary*, s.v. "honour."
3. Ibrahim, *A Brief Illustrated Guide to Understanding Islam*, 61.
4. Brummer, *Atonement, Christology and the Trinity*, 69, 74–75.

intellectual abilities, growing influence as a teacher and spiritual director meant that when Lanfranc moved to Canterbury to become archbishop, Anselm was appointed abbot. It was not something he desired.[5] He only wanted to pray and teach. His years at Bec were happy ones. He inspired the novices, penned many letters and began writing significant theological treatises. When Lanfranc died in 1089 the English clergy wanted him as their archbishop. Again Anselm refused. In any case King William Rufus was opposed to Anselm's appointment—the king wanted control. Only when the king was seriously ill did he give way and a reluctant Anselm was invested by force.

A falling-out between Anselm and the king was inevitable. In 1097 Anselm was forced to leave the country. After Rufus's death in 1100 he was welcomed back by the new king, Henry I, only to be again driven into exile because of a flaring up of conflict between monarch and archbishop. This tension between church and state was to culminate sixty years later in the murder of another Primate—Thomas Becket.

From the above we can see that Anselm's thinking was shaped by two all absorbing institutions. One was the monastery in whose ordered existence he found happiness and the other the feudal world of northern Europe. Both were hierarchical.[6] These two institutions held back the forces of lawlessness, barbarism, brutality, and chaos. At the top of the ecclesiastical world was the pope then a descending escalator of archbishops, bishops, priors, monks, and laypeople, each linked to his superior through a chain of obedience and submission. Similarly at the pinnacle of the feudal system was the king followed by barons, knights, and freemen with serfs at the bottom. The glue binding the structures together was the construct of honor.

As already stated, each theory of atonement and every jeweled metaphor has a historical, political, geographical, and social context. Anselm viewed God's relationship with human beings in terms of a lord dealing with his vassals.

---

5. Evans, *Anselm*, 19.
6. Dillistone, *The Christian Understanding of the Atonement*, 191.

The Wrath of God Satisfied?

CUR DEUS HOMO

Anselm's great work on the atonement *Cur Deus Homo* was completed in exile. People throughout the ages have stumbled over the scandalous nature of the cross. Anselm writes to answer the objections of "infidels" (presumably Jews and Muslims) who thought the idea of God becoming a man to suffer and die was unseemly.

Even though Anselm's name is linked with a theory, *Cur Deus Homo* does not set out a theory. Instead, the forty-seven chapters of his two-volume-exposition take the reader on a prayerful journey from faith to understanding. The "infidels" are not addressed directly. Instead Anselm engages in a dialogue with Boso—a monk of questioning faith—who in later years also became Abbot of Bec. Anselm uses the teacher's method of "question and answer." From the outset Anselm sets the issue of God's honor within the divine attributes of compassion, love, and tenderness.

> *Boso.* Infidels ridiculing our simplicity, charge upon us that we do injustice and dishonor to God when we affirm that he descended into the womb of a virgin . . . grew on the nourishment of milk . . . endured fatigue, hunger . . . and crucifixion among thieves.
>
> *Anselm.* We do no injustice or dishonor to God but give him thanks with all the heart praising and proclaiming the ineffable height of his compassion. For the more astonishing a thing it is and beyond expectation, that he has restored us; . . . by so much the more has he shown his more exceeding love and tenderness towards us.[7]

Anselm refutes the suggestion that angels could have rescued humankind. He also dismisses the classical idea of "Christ the Victor" so that Satan is put right out of the picture.[8] Following Paul in Romans 1:21, Anselm defines sin as the refusal to give honor to God. Anselm then pastes this definition into his own feudal context, using inherited ideas of debt and satisfaction.

> *Boso.* What is the debt which we owe God?
>
> *Anselm.* This is justice, or uprightness of will . . . this is the sole and complete debt of honour . . . which God requires of us . . . He who does not render this honour which is due to God, robs God

---

7. *CDH*.1/III.
8. Evans, *Anselm*, 74.

of his own and dishonours him; and this is sin. Moreover, so long as he (man) does not restore what he has taken away, he remains in fault; . . . so he who violates another's honour . . . must according to the extent of the injury done, make restoration in some way satisfactory to the person he has dishonoured.[9]

The debt is so vast that neither men nor angels can pay it. Only God can restore honor to God. Jesus Christ—the God-Man (*Deus Homo*)—becomes incarnate to "satisfy" this debt.

TERTULLIAN'S LEGACY

The idea of satisfaction had been around for more than eight hundred years. While Irenaeus was fighting against persecution and heresy in Lyon, Tertullian (160–225), a converted pagan from Carthage, was busy defending the Old Testament and formulating a doctrine of the Trinity. His legal training was to help him defend the church and deal with difficult pastoral matters.

How should Christians, who had fallen from faith during persecution, be treated? This pastoral question taxed Tertullian's ingenuity. Should these backsliders be readmitted to the church or excluded? Other questions are linked. How big is the sin of apostasy compared with other sins? If apostates are to be allowed back what penalty should be imposed as a penance? Should they be punished or could some satisfactory compensation be made? Could the accumulated merit of the martyrs (like Irenaeus) be used to repay the debt of those who had defaulted? With such ideas circulating it is easy to see how legal terminology was to exert a malign influence upon atonement theories.

Ideas of debt, merit, and satisfaction were useful tools for Archbishop Anselm when challenged by the pastoral and political problems of his day. Disagreements between a lord and a vassal could be resolved if an imposed satisfaction was paid to the feudal lord.

DIVINE CHILD ABUSE

Anselm's theory that the Father sent the Son to make "a satisfaction" on our behalf draws criticisms from feminist theologians who see

9. CDH.1/XI, 215.

Anselm's God as a "status-paranoid power-monger who deliberately humiliates and infantilizes human beings."[10] If God sacrifices his son to satisfy his honor, isn't this divine child abuse? Shadows of the punitive father and merciless tyrant haunt images of forgiving grace.[11]

It is not easy to get around the abuse charge, nor should we try since God "did not withhold his own Son but gave him up for all of us" (Rom 8:32). Anselm, however, insists that the Father did not compel or manipulate his Son into suffering. Christ freely chose the vocation of a victim.[12]

> *Anselm.* (Christ) suffered death of his own will . . . He speaks of the will of the Father, not because the Father preferred the death of the Son to his life . . . 'I lay down my own life that I may take it again; no man taketh it from me, but I lay it down of myself.'[13]

Although this may go some way in repudiating the charge of divine child abuse, feminist theologians from their studies of domestic violence have highlighted other problems.[14]

Although Christ chooses to be a tortured victim is there not something voyeuristic and disturbing when another family member watches pain being inflicted? Boso in *Cur Deus Homo* recognizes the difficulty.

> *Boso.* But this simple fact, that God allows him to be so treated, even if he were willing, does not seem becoming for such a Father in respect to such a Son.[15]

Anselm responds to Boso's comment by pointing to the integrity of the Trinity. He describes a conversation taking place between Father, Son, and Spirit. What I find surprising is the lack of any hierarchical ordering within these Trinitarian relationships. This is remarkable given the feudal context from which he is writing. Anselm's Trinity presents us with the astonishing insight—which we shall explore in part two—that through mutual sharing and participation between Father and Son, God the Father demonstrates himself to be both the "victor" and the "victim." A similar interactive mutuality within the Trinity works with the issue of honour.

---

10. Ray, *Deceiving the Devil*, 51.
11. Ibid., 8–11.
12. *CDH*, 1/IX.
13. *CDH*, 1/VIII.
14. Ray, *Deceiving the Devil*, 59.
15. *CDH*, 1/X.

> *Anselm.* That honor certainly belongs to the whole Trinity; and since he (Christ) is very God, he offered himself for his own honour, as well as for that of the Father and the Holy Spirit; that is, he gave his humanity to his divinity, which is one person of the Trinity.[16]

THE HONOR AND THE ASEITY OF GOD

Unfortunately Anselm keeps the humanity of Jesus and the divinity of the Father at arms length. He inherits from the Church Fathers a metaphysical understanding of deity. God is omnipotent (all-powerful), omniscient (all-seeing), omnipresent (present everywhere). Even the concept of "existence" had become a metaphysical category of deity for Anselm. Furthermore his God is "unchangeable" with a divine nature that is "impassible"[17]—a word suggesting that God is incapable of feeling or suffering.

Divinity is therefore placed in a protective plastic bubble. God, the "feudal" Lord, remains untouched by the anguish of his Son. Anselm attaches a further quality to his metaphysical Trinity. The technical term "aseity" describes God's self-sufficiency. It suggests that God remains unaffected by the actions of human beings. If this is so, why does Anselm make so much fuss about God's honor being damaged by human beings? He is not unmindful of the question.

> *Anselm.* Nothing can be added to or taken from the honour of God . . . But when he (man) does not choose what he ought . . . he disturbs the order and beauty of the universe, as relates to himself, although he cannot injure nor tarnish the power and majesty of God.[18]

God's honour is demonstrated, replicated, and enacted in creation. Although God in his nature is unaffected, creation is and therefore we are! In a roundabout way Anselm is arguing that Christ came to suffer and die in order to prevent the natural order of things collapsing around us. Richard Southern in his important work on Anselm concludes, "Regarded in

---

16. *CDH*, 2/XVIII.
17. *CDH*, 1/VIII.
18. *CDH*, 1/XV.

The Wrath of God Satisfied?

this way, God's honor is simply another word for the ordering of the universe in its due relationship with God".[19]

Anselm is telling us that without the atonement, human violence would destroy the ecclesiastical and feudal systems of his time, which are visible manifestations of God's honor. These medieval institutions, in spite of their deficiencies, protected civilization from barbarism, rape, and pillage, and alleviated some of the effects of natural disaster. Without atonement, civilization would perish. His atonement theory is institutional and ecological!

FROM HUBRIS TO NEMESIS

Anselm's insight has an immediate application for our contemporary institutions of government and banking. Both, like secularized forms of the feudal system, are meant to guard and enhance the lives of the people they serve.

Karl Barth argues, "Without God's honor there is no honor for man, no human worth or dignity."[20] All who forget this, like reckless bankers and dishonorable politicians, not only destroy their own standing but also that of the institutions they represent. Our vocation is to participate in God's honor. This we do through our service to him and to others (John 12:26).

The stability of any country or community is maintained either by a culture of law or a culture of honor. Anselm's feudal system with its principle of satisfaction is a mixture of both.[21] The concept of honor survives in tribal communities and also in what have been described as "hot-blooded" cultures.[22] These lie around the Mediterranean Sea, most of the Arab world, and some of the countries of the Far East. These cultures have also been transmitted by conquest and emigration to the Americas. When honor disappears then civilized life will only be maintained by a system of law. Countries under pressure to effect a rapid cultural transition from one to the other—like Iraq and Afghanistan—have real difficulties.

19. Southern, *St. Anselm*, 226.
20. Barth, *CD* 3/4, 685.
21. Dillistone, *The Christian Understanding of the Atonement*, 193.
22. http://en.wikipedia.org/wike/honour.

Dishonorable Dealings

Vince Cable, in his analysis of Britain's "credit-crunch" sees Mrs. Thatcher's financial reforms of the 1980s radically changing the high-streets banks from being "safe but boring to being aggressively competitive and less secure."[23] He argues that anyone with a grasp of history will know that individual and collective stupidity, greed, and complacency, is a recurrent feature of every civilization. Credit-crunch was able to happen because honor within the banking industry had disappeared and the regulation of law ineffective. Cable says, "the amoral, cynical financial dealings which, we were assured, created wealth have not only contributed to instability but to a weakening of the wider social contract."[24] Presumption has ended in retribution, or in Cable's words: "hubris is giving way to nemesis."[25] This was Anselm's concern.

There is an immediate application to the "no blame/no shame" culture of the House of Commons. Some Members of Parliament had obviously forgotten they were "honorable" members and had interpreted "the rules" in a very lax way. Five months on, one of the MPs is said to have recanted. "I feel honor-bound to pay this money back." Others, in both Houses of Parliament, remained convinced that they had done nothing wrong and continued the rhetoric of self-justification.

ANSELM'S POSITIVE LEGACY

Anselm's "satisfaction" theory was forged in a patriarchal and feudal society. Difficulties always occur when one attempts to lift a theory from one context and paste it into a different time and place. As spelled out in chapter 1, atonement theories are contextual and utilitarian.

Although the concept of law and satisfaction does infiltrate his thinking, Anselm did not set his atonement theory within the courtroom like some of the Protestant Reformers. He would probably not subscribe to the line "the wrath of God is satisfied." His concern was not with wrath but with honor. Honor protects civilization from barbarism. His medieval world was not held together by legal codes but by the quality of the relationship between lord and vassal. It was certainly hierarchical, but it was shaped by covenantal rather than by contractual ideas.

23. Cable, *The Storm*, 52.
24. Ibid., 157.
25. Ibid., 1.

The Wrath of God Satisfied?

Anselm was wrestling with problems not unlike our own: institutional insecurity, violence, and debt. His solution lay not in more regulation but in gift. Because we have disabled ourselves with debt, God has to bail us out.[26] God's honor gift in Jesus Christ is not simply a repayment to extract us from moral credit-crunch; his gift is far more generous.[27] While "satisfaction" may not have a contemporary resonance, the question of "debt" certainly does—as we shall see in the final chapter.

The second volume of *Cur Deus Homo* concentrates on the "up-side" of this by focusing on the extravagance of God's gift. Boso, like every good scholar, wants to know more.

> *Boso*. I wish you would go further with me, and enable me to understand . . .
>
> *Anselm*. Rational nature was made holy, in order to be happy in enjoying the supreme good, which is God. Therefore man . . . was made holy for this end, that he might be happy in enjoying God.[28]

Human beings are made for happiness and holiness. Although Anselm believed in the wondrous love of God, it was Abelard—whom we shall meet in the next chapter—who majored on this theme.[29]

---

26. *CDH*, 1/XXIV.
27. Sykes, *The Story of Atonement*, 35.
28. *CDH*, 2/I.
29. Schmiechen, *Saving Power*, 290.

5

Love Moved Him to Die

THE YEAR WAS 1958. It was Passion Sunday. I went along to the City Temple in London[1] and joined the queue waiting to enter the church for the evening service. It was always packed when Leslie Weatherhead was the preacher.[2]

I vividly recall the impact of his sermon. His quiet hypnotic voice, so musical in tone, helped us "to see Jesus" and feel the power of his dying love. Many of us in the congregation wept as we sang the closing hymn.

> When I survey the wondrous cross,
> On which the Prince of Glory died,
> My richest gain I count but loss,
> And pour contempt on all my pride.[3]

The sermon—based on Matthew 23:37—had begun in an easy conversational style. Profound theological truth was presented in such a way that its emotional impact drew the congregation to the foot of the cross. Weatherhead's closing illustration described a situation with which I could readily identify.[4]

> There was young man who longed to escape from his small town. He wanted to see 'real life.' 'I'm sick of this place' he kept saying

---

1. Situated on the Holborn Viaduct in the City of London, it was regarded by many as the cathedral of the Congregational Church.
2. Morris, *Snapshots*, 81.
3. *MHB*, 182.
4. Stuckey, *On the Edge of Pentecost,* 26–27.

to his recently bereaved mother. There was no hesitation when a friend invited him to live in London. Months went by. Occasionally his mother received a note—usually requesting money. After nine months all communication ceased. His mother was worried, not only because of her own terminal cancer, but because she knew her son's character. At last a minister tracked him down and told him to go home because his mother was ill. Nothing happened. Finally a telegram: 'Your mother is dying!' The son came home but it was too late. He climbed the narrow stairway of his boyhood home, entered his mother's low-ceiling bedroom. There lay her lifeless body. When he saw the stricken face, the shrunken form and the snow-white hair, he fell sobbing at the bedside. She had loved him so much. Why hadn't he come home?[5]

Dramatic! Theatrical! Yes. Few in the congregation could fail to make the connection between this story and the story of God's patient suffering love.

THE MESSAGE OF LOVE

The explanations of Irenaeus, Athanasius, and Anselm can seem too complicated for many church-goers who may ask, "Is not the love of God the heart of the Christian message?" Karl Barth—best known for his many volumes of *Church Dogmatics*—was asked before a distinguished company of scholars, "what is your greatest theological insight?" He paused for a moment before replying, "Jesus loves me, this I know, for the Bible tells me so".[6]

Throughout the Old Testament God never stops loving his recalcitrant people. Even when sent into exile he tries to show them that love is stronger than death.[7] Jesus, in the New Testament, extends this love story to all humanity through his portrayal of God as a universal Father who "makes his sun rise on the evil and the good" (Matt 5:45). Nowhere is this message more powerfully expressed than in the parable of the lost son (Luke 15:11–37).

Leslie Weatherhead was following the story-telling example of Jesus. He was also the final pulpit flourish of a strand of atonement thinking

---

5. Author's recounting.
6. Chalk and Mann, *Lost Message of Jesus*, 46.
7. Stuckey, *Into the Far Country*, 48–50.

that had gained ground following the "Enlightment" of the seventeeth century and the rise of Methodism in the eighteenth. This experiential message of the "wondrous love of God" permeates the hymns of Charles Wesley.

> Love moved him to die,
> And on this we rely;
> He hath loved, He hath loved us; we cannot tell why; [8]

New Testament scholars, during the nineteenth century, sought to rescue Jesus from the theological and institutional captivity of the church. Romanticism was infecting the culture. Traditional atonement theories with their metaphysical language were to acquire a more mystical and emotional emphasis. F. D. Schleiermacher (1768–1834) was the first to expound the atonement message psychologically, rather than philosophically, or dogmatically.[9] Christians looked to the example of Jesus and his self-giving love. Cecil Alexander's popular hymn "There is a green hill"— first published in 1848—sums up the mood of the time.

> O dearly, dearly has He loved,
> And we must love him too,
> And trust in his redeeming blood,
> And try his works to do.[10]

When idealism and optimism permeate a culture, "love" becomes the dominant atonement metaphor.

PETER ABELARD

The message of transforming love had been proclaimed 860 years before Weatherhead by another preacher who drew the crowds. His name was Peter Abelard (1079–1142). To him has been attributed the "moral influence" theory of atonement.

In the late 1120s he was the rising star of the University of Paris. His brilliant lectures and charismatic personality drew students from afar. He was the pupil who, without previous training, outstripped the masters. Medieval theologians like Anselm had said, "I must believe in

8. *MHB*, 66.
9. Dillistone, *The Christian Understanding of the Atonement*, 338–340.
10. *MHB*, 180.

order to understand." Abelard took the opposite course. "I must understand in order to believe." This got him into trouble with the authorities. His problems were compounded by his "affair" with Heloise—one of his students. A secret marriage was proposed. Heloise escape to the convent of Argenteuil and was forced to become a nun—a vocation for which she had no calling. Fulbert—a powerful canon of Notre-Dame—blamed it all on Abelard and had him castrated. This ended his ecclesiastical career.

The remaining twenty-three years of his life were marked by turmoil, pain, and conflict. Not authorised to lecture and finding no respite in the cloister, he began to teach and write unofficially. His enemies were incensed. Charges were brought. He escaped and hid in the forest as a hermit. Students from Paris nevertheless discovered were he was and flocked to him. An alternative theological community—the Oratory of the Paraclete—was formed. He again fled from persecution. His one consolation was Heloise. The spiritual bond between them has become the stuff of romantic legend.[11] Abelard's final years were plagued with trials and accusations.

THE GREAT THAW

Anselm's context was monastic and feudal. God is the "overlord" whose honor must be safeguarded. For Abelard, God was the "Divine Lover." Abelard lived in what has been described as "the great thaw"—one of those periods in history when warmth and confidence touches frozen humanity.[12] In Western Europe around 1100 there was an extraordinary outpouring of energy. People set off on pilgrimages and crusades. Towering cathedrals started to soar above the landscape. Cold brutality was on the wane and a new era of courtly love was dawning to culminate in the lives of Christians like Saint Francis. Abelard was the first fruiting of this new context.

Anselm in his prayers to Mary, the mother of Jesus, had expressed himself in a very intimate way.[13] Now, the language of love in Christian devotion becomes commonplace.

---

11. Waddel, *Peter Abelard*.
12. *Civilization: A Personal View* by Kenneth Clark, 23.
13. Anselm, "A prayer to St Mary," 207.

Love Moved Him to Die

For Abelard the love of God was no empty abstraction. It is given real content in the life and work of Jesus.[14] Moreover his death was not simply a revelation of love, Christ died so that God's love could be actively poured into us repairing our nature.[15]

> Art thou not moved to tears . . . He, the only-begotten of God, was killed for thy sake, as an offering, of His own will. Over Him, not another, let thy sorrow be in entering into His sufferings, and enter into His suffering by sorrow! . . . He is the true lover, who longs for thyself, not for anything that is thine. He is the true friend, who said Himself, when ready to die for thee, 'Greater love hath no man than this, that a man lay down his life for his friends.'[16]

This is a quotation taken from a letter Abelard wrote to Heloise. One cannot fail to notice the experiential connection between Abelard's theological views and his passionate relationship with her. Victor Murray writes, "As a human being the most outstanding thing in Abelard's experience was the unselfish, passionate, disinterested love shown to him by Heloise. The characteristic thing in his theology was his emphasis on the unselfish love of God inflaming the soul."[17]

A RADICAL DEPARTURE

Like Anselm, Abelard removed Satan from the drama of atonement.[18] Because our salvation is rooted in God's eternal election, the devil poses no threat. Abelard also undercuts Anselm's argument about God requiring a debt payment. "How cruel and wicked it seems that anyone should demand the blood of an innocent person as the price of anything." [19] The concept of satisfaction is also dismissed.[20] The life, death, and resurrection of Jesus is simply a straightforward proclamation of love.

> Christ has fully bound us to himself by love; with the result that our hearts should be enkindled by such a gift of divine grace, and

14. Weingart, *The Logic of Divine Love*, 121.
15. Fiddes, *Past Event and Present Salvation*, 144–145.
16. Quoted in Moberly, *Atonement and Personality*, 377–378.
17. Quoted in Walters, "The Atonement in Medieval Theology," 246.
18. Weingart, *The Logic of Divine Love*, 121.
19. Ray, *Deceiving the Devil*, 13.
20. Weingard, *The Logic of Divine Love*, 142.

> true charity should not now shrink from enduring anything for him ... So does he bear witness that he came for the express purpose of spreading his true liberty of love amongst men?[21]

Abelard has been accused of holding a mere exemplary view of atonement. Certainly he does exhort us to imitate Christ, but there is more. Christ dies so that the love of God can 'be poured out in our hearts'. As Athanasius had taught; a process of divinisation was as work repairing our natures and drawing us from corruption to incorruption.

> Dispelling our shadows with light, he showed us both by his words and example, the fullness of all virtues and repaired our nature.[22]

Because Abelard emphasized personal experience, his theory has been described as "subjective" over and against Anselm's "objective" view of atonement.[23] Such labelling, although convenient, is inaccurate. Abelard's description of our hearts being "inflamed," "enkindled," and "repaired" tell us that Christ not only influences us morally but effects real change in us through his Spirit.

Sadly Abelard's teaching failed to have a lasting impact even though it resonated with the context and culture of the time. Why was this? According to Diarmaid MacCulloch, great changes in authority, power, and regulation were taking place through the Gregorian reforms. A "new aggressiveness" was appearing in Christian spirituality.[24] The latter was given militant expression in the crusades and in the church's fanatical suppression of heresy. It is here that the austere figure of Bernard of Clairvaux—Abelard's severest critic—steps onto the stage.[25]

With unbounded energy he stormed around preaching "crusade" and like a "true knight of courtly love" had his own lady—the Virgin Mary. His intimate and mystical spirituality filters down to us in a hymn like "Jesus, the very thought of Thee, with sweetness fills my breast."[26] Unfortunately he had the vices of a passionate man who knows he is always right.[27] This gave him "thug-like" qualities as a churchman. Believing

21. Abelard, "Exposition of Romans 3:19," 280.
22. Fiddes, *Past Event and Present Salvation*, 145.
23. Brunner, *The Mediator*, 439–445.
24. MacCulloch, *Christian History*, 134.
25. Underhill, *The Mystics of the Church*, 88.
26. *MHB*, 108.
27. Gascoine, *The Christians*, 78.

Love Moved Him to Die

Abelard's rational inquiry destroyed faith, Bernard made it his mission to seek out, destroy, and obliterate his influence. Abelard would not be rehabilitated until romantic individualism again blossomed and open theological enquiry became an acceptable approach to faith as described above.

THE VOCATION OF A VICTIM

In spite of his stress on the love of God, Abelard's writings still contain the traditional jewel-like metaphors of sacrifice, purchase, penalty, curse, wrath, and victory.[28] He remains imprisoned within the metaphysical categories he had inherited. He also seemed to be suggesting that victims should accept their fate.

> Think on him always, sister . . . Keep him in mind. Look at him going to be crucified for your sake, carrying his own cross. Be one of the crowd, one of the women who wept and lamented over him.[29]

Heloise is being exhorted to identify with Christ and accept her suffering. Although such passivity is developed in Ignatian spirituality, some today find it unacceptable.[30]

Because the resurrection is God's "signature across the life and death of Jesus,"[31] his early life should not be regarded as an unimportant prelude to the main action which takes place on the cross. From this it can then be argued that Jesus died not because he was passive, but because he choose to confront evil, and therefore suffered the terrible consequences of such an active vocation.[32]

IS LOVE ENOUGH?

Abelard in his commentary on Romans writes of the change which takes place when a person experiences the love of God. "Every man is made

---

28. Fiddes, *Past Event and Present Salvation*, 156–157.
29. Abelard, *Letters*, 150–151.
30. Ray, *Deceiving the Devil*, 70.
31. Richardson, *Paul for Today*, 78.
32. Ray, *Deceiving the Devil*, 138.

more just, more loving towards God . . . that great love for us shown in the Passion of Christ . . . frees us from the bondage of sin."[33]

This was Weatherhead's message. Although his illustration of the young man sobbing by the bedside suggests contrition, one must ask whether it led to real repentance and a subsequent transformation? As we sang Isaac Watts hymn "When I survey the wondrous cross" some of us wept but did the emotional impact effect a lasting change in us? Does experiencing selfless love remove sin? It depends on how sin is defined.

For Abelard, sin is something which distances a person from God creating human dysfunction and confusion. It obstructs but does not negate the good. For Anselm, sin has an objective reality. It stands as a tangible barrier separating persons and communities from each other. It drives a wedge between humanity and God. It therefore has to be forcibly removed. If it is not destroyed, it will destroy. Abelard's understanding reflects the context of courtly love. Anselm addresses the brutal realities of violence. For Abelard, Christ through his teaching, his example, his life and his death illuminates and repairs. For Anselm, God in Christ exercises invasive surgery to remove a toxic reality which negates and destroys. Does Abelard take sin seriously enough? Do recipients of selfless love always become better people?

Bernice and Terry had fostered children for forty-five years. They had also brought up five children of their own, two of whom had Down's syndrome. They agreed to look after twelve-year-old Harry for two weekends. Harry was with them for over a year because his previous foster family refused to have him back. During that time Harry stole from them, broke into cars, was a persistent shop-lifter, and drenched their home with water. They requested information from Social Services about Harry's background and appealed for support. Little was offered and the case worker was usually unavailable. When they finally saw Harry's files they were horrified. There had been a history of sexual abuse, traumatic neglect, and evidence of sexual advances towards other children. They immediately feared for their own children, wondering if Harry had abused them.

This was one of several stories reported by the Press in September 2009. Stories about the recurring absence of support and information given to those fostering disturbed children had become newsworthy because

---

33. Dillistone, *The Christian Understanding of the Atonement*, 326.

of a terrifying incident in Edlington, England, in which two brothers aged ten and eleven, also fostered, had brutally attacked two other children with knives, bricks, and burning cigarettes. In the ensuing correspondence one foster parent wrote, "I always thought love would be enough, I now know it is not."

The belief that love is enough runs into difficulties when we examine other cases; Judas, the apostle, being a prime example.

> So when he (Jesus) had dipped the piece of bread, he gave it to Judas son of Simon Iscariot. After he had received the piece of bread, Satan entered into him . . . he immediately went out. And it was night. (John 13:26–30).

Judas is a blot on the Christian landscape of love. The Gospel of John attempts an explanation as some still do.[34] While money may have been a factor, John's Gospel makes it clear that Judas represents the dark side of the cosmos. Jesus has already washed the feet of his trusted friend and now gives him the choicest morsel of food. He may even have placed it in Judas' mouth as a token of special love.[35] For those trapped in the labyrinth of sin, love can repel and trigger a violent response.

A LEGACY OF LOVE

Abelard was a blazing comet who left a trail of love. According to R. C Moberley:

> Incomplete and imperfectly consistent though his teaching was, it contained beyond all question, the germ . . . of an exposition of the atonement far deeper and more inclusive than that of the theologians who condemned him.[36]

First, Abelard opened up a new way of looking at things by adopting a theological method radically different from Anselm. By starting with a person's attempt to understand rather than the declared faith of the church one can see why he was a threat to the ecclesiastical authorities.

> He fought against ignorance, against hypocrisy, against spiritual sloth, against an easy faith that was the faith of gulls and not men.

34. Paffenroth, *Judas*.
35. Vanier, *Drawn into the Mystery of Jesus*, 242.
36. Moberley, *Atonement and Personality*, 373.

> He had written for his young men, calling them to doubt, arming them against the deadlier sin of dullness.[37]

Second, although Abelard's theory succeeds in removing the charge of "divine child abuse," he has separated the divine initiative of the Father from the actual death of Christ. The scandalous insistence of the New Testament that the son of man "must undergo great suffering," and "and be killed" (Mark 8:31), should not be removed lest we loose an indispensable feature of atonement—namely justice.[38]

Third, Abelard prompts us to follow Christ's example of living out the text "No one has greater love than this, to lay down one's life for one's friends" (John 15:12). This return to Jesus and the ethic of love has inspired many who seek liberation for the oppressed. It is well expressed by Martin Luther King:

> We shall match your capacity to inflict suffering by our capacity to endure suffering . . . Throw us into jail, and we shall still love you. Send your hooded perpetrators of violence into our community at the midnight hour and beat us and leave us half dead, and we shall still love you.[39]

Fourth, while singular examples of self-giving love do illuminate our dark world, do such sacrifices make a lasting difference? In a violent world, such as ours today, naked power, abuse, torture, crime, disaster and curruption hit the headlines. Weatherhead and Abelard belong to a more gentle nostaligic age where everyone "lives happily ever after."

Ours is an age of violence, threat, and economic insecurity. It is not easy retaining Abelard's optimism. Can we still hold fast to his vision of love? Our next chapter suggests that we can and should.

---

37. Waddel, *Peter Abelard*, 263.

38. This divine "must" will be examined in our next chapter. The issue of divine necessity and justice will occupy our attention in part two.

39. King, *Strength to Love*, 54.

6

Too Much Blood

On Tuesday the twelfth of January 2010 an earthquake of catastrophic magnitude rent the island of Haiti. It was estimated that 230,000 people were killed and 300,000 injured. Initial pictures showed buildings reduced to rubble and notable landmarks destroyed. Over a million people suddenly became homeless without food and water. The total infrastructure was obliterated. Government was unable to function; roads were impassable, transport facilities, hospitals, and electrical networks disabled. All this hampered rescue efforts. Although many countries responded immediately sending food, medical teams, and engineers, confusion over who was in charge and problems of distribution complicated early relief work. Delays in aid distribution led to angry scenes of looting and violence. A hospital worker when interviewed said, "It is like working in a war situation. We don't have any more morphine to manage pain for our patients. We cannot accept that planes carrying lifesaving medical supplies and equipment continue to be turned away while our patients die."

Many of us witnessed the unfolding drama on television, listened to the stories of survivors, and saw bodies dragged from the ruins. By the twenty-second of January the search for those buried beneath the fallen masonry was finally called off, yet even after that date a few, who somehow managed to live buried beneath the tons of rubble, were dug out to the jubilation of those who persisted in looking for loved ones. One enduring image is of a group of survivors standing in the ruins of a church weeping, worshipping, and pouring out their praises to God.

The Wrath of God Satisfied?

Haiti is a country where the colonizers created discord between the black inhabitants and reduced them to slavery. The latter had made many attempts to liberate themselves and finally succeeded in 1803. Yet justice continued to escape them. The history of Haiti is littered with dictatorships, abandoned elections, uprisings, burnings, and beatings. Even in 1987 the stealing, killing, and raping continued. The 1991 coup was one of the bloodiest of all where, in a reign of terror, the army killed over 10,000 people. In spite of the deposed President's return in 1994 injustice remains endemic. Haiti's difficulties continued even after the earthquake as Aid agencies raced to prevent cholera reaching a million homeless people. Can the little group who sang in the ruins of a church still believe that one day all shall be well for their country?

Abelard's message of atonement as self-giving-love was voiced in the optimistic culture of courtly love. In this chapter we explore how the message of love was expressed in a context of political, economic, and social upheaval, and natural disaster. In a context, where people suffer and die from calamity and war, the primary metaphors are "blood" and "sacrifice." The word "sacrifice" is derived from two Latin words: *sacer*—"holy," and *facere*—"to make." Can the cross "make whole" a country that continues to bleed?

ANOTHER DISASTER ZONE

Norwich—on the East coast of England—was a city of growing wealth in the fourteenth century. Not all was well however. The Black Death visited Norwich in 1349. Estimates of those who died in his epidemic and in the two that followed were put at 2,400 out of a total population of 6,000.[1] The main victims of the 1362 plague were children. In that same year, a great gale blow down the cathedral spire, uprooted trees, and damaged houses. This was followed by an infectious disease that destroyed the cattle. For the next three years the harvest failed. Finally all the money ran out. Hunger and desperation sparked the Peasants' Revolt of 1381 in which churches were looted and monasteries despoiled. The insurrection was savagely put down by the Bishop of Norwich; the leaders were hung, drawn and quartered. This was also the time of the Great Schism when the Roman Church was scandalously torn apart by two rival Popes.

1. Upjohn, *In Search of Julian of Norwich*, 24.

The church was corrupt, the monasteries depleted, and the ecclesiastical authorities busy trying to ban the new Bible and exterminate the faithful followers of John Wyclif. The smell of burning bodies and death was commonplace in Norwich.

> And all his disciples, and all those who truly love him, suffered greater pain than they would for their own bodily death . . . Either the world is coming to an end, or else he who made all nature is suffering.[2]

These remarkable words were spoken by a woman who uttered the famous words, "All shall be well". Her name is unknown. We only know she lived in a cell built on the side of the Church of St. Julian.

TOO MUCH BLOOD

When Julian was thirty years old, she was struck down with a serious illness. Expecting to die she received the rites of the church, but lingered for several days. When her breathing started to fail a priest was sent for. He held a crucifix before her and commanded her to look at it, since she had turned her eyes upwards to heaven. When she fixed her eyes upon the cross, all the pain suddenly left her. She thought this to be the moment of death. Then something horrifying happened to the crucifix.

> I saw red blood trickling down from under the crown of thorns, all hot, freshly, plentifully and vividly, just as I imagined it was at the moment when the crown of thorns was thrust on to his blessed head.[3]

> The great drops fell . . . like pellets, as though they had come out of the veins; the blood was very thick; and as it spread it was bright red . . . horrifying and awe-inspiring, sweet and lovely.[4]

The very idea that such a sight could be "sweet and lovely" is difficult for those church-goers who no longer have "faith in his blood"—to use Cranmer's gritty phrase—or who recoil from singing William Cowper's hymn:

> There is a fountain filled with blood.

2. Julian, *Revelations of Divine Love*, LT.18, 67–68.
3. Ibid., ST.1, 6.
4. Ibid., LT.7, 50–51.

> Drawn from Immanuel's veins:
> And sinner, plunged beneath that flood,
> Lose all their guilty stains.[5]

Julian further describes her blood soaked vision in graphic detail.

> After this I saw, as I watched, the body of Christ bleeding abundantly, in wheals from the scourging. It looked like this: the fair skin was deeply broken, down into the tender flesh, sharply slashed all over the dear body; the hot blood ran so abundantly that no skin or wound could be seen, it seemed to be all blood. And it looked so abundant to me that I thought if at that moment it had been real natural blood, the whole bed would have been blood-soaked and even the floor around . . . Because of the tender love he has for us, yet it pleases him better that we should simply take his holy blood to wash away our sins.[6]

BLOOD SACRIFICES

Sin leaves a stain. If a wife discovers that her husband has been unfaithful he will seem stained in her eyes even after he has confessed and sought to make restitution. If human beings are to move on, after committing a major transgression, they need to participate in some act of "cleansing." What is polluted can be restored through contact with something whole (holy) and clean. This idea lies behind the purification rituals of the Day of Atonement, sacrifice, and the laying-on of hands. Jesus, within his ministry, repeatedly reaches out to "touch" the unclean, remove shame, and restore that person to the community.[7]

Frances Young, in her exposition of the different Old Testament sacrifices, argues that the sacrifice of animals (Lev16:3–28, 23:9–21), which took place on the Day of Atonement, really came to prominence after the Babylonian exile and was a type of "super-sin-offering." The potency of a sacrifice depended upon the ritual and the attitude of the person making the offering. She reminds us that many of the routine sacrifices were offerings from the earth like grain, oil, and honey. Nevertheless, animals

---

5. *MHB*, 201.
6. Julian, *Revelations of Divine Love*, LT.12, 59.
7. Goldingay, "Old Testament Sacrifice and the Death of Christ," 11.

were sacrificed as "guilt offerings" and were believed to effect atonement in cases of "gross neglect."[8]

Some argue that atoning sacrifices make things right by demanding the payment of a penalty to "make satisfaction." This averts God's "wrath and curse" so that he can again bless.[9] Others argue that, when an animal was sacrificed, it was *not* to propitiate God but rather to express thanksgiving to God though a shared communal feast.[10] Even the Passover sacrifices can to be viewed as acts of thanksgiving that identify Israel with the liberating event of the Exodus. Is "sacrifice" the seal of a relationship or the means to it?[11] This question brings us back to the dilemma stated in chapter 1. Is atonement about expiation or propitiation?

The Old Testament prophets counterbalanced the "priestly tradition" by emphasizing how sacrificial ritual was useless unless accompanied by moral virtue. They insisted on the superiority of justice, mercy, and love over all forms of material offering. They did not, however, advocate the complete rejection of ritual sacrifices. While the Old Testament, apart from a few examples (2 Sam 24), does not view "blood letting" as a means of buying off the anger of God, nevertheless in the words of Young: "The wrath of God was not to be treated lightly. This is the sort of theology which molded the ritual of the Priestly Code. God causes punishment for sin; God alone can get rid of sin; God gave sacrifice as a ritual means of dealing with sin."[12]

We should not, therefore, "rub out" references to "blood," or rule out the idea of "propitiation." Jesus is the "high priest" who makes "a sacrifice of atonement for the sins of the people" (Heb 2:17).[13]

> Jesus understood his own person and work to be a replacement—or rather, fulfillment—of everything that Israel's temple had been and done. Jesus' words during the Last Supper suggest that he substituted his own person and work for the temple and its sacrificial system.[14]

8. Thompson, *Where is the God of Justice?*, 95–96.
9. Barnes, *Atonement Matters*, 55.
10. Young, *Sacrifice and the Death of Christ*, 28.
11. Goldingay, 6.
12. Young, *Sacrifice and the Death of Christ*, 32.
13. The verb can be translated either "expiation" or "propitiation."
14. Vanhoozer, "The Atonement in Postmodernity," 397–400.

The Wrath of God Satisfied?

Mel Gibson's film, *The Passion of Christ,* glories in blood. It spatters the assailants as chunks of flesh are torn away in the flogging. The Latin word *satis* ("enough"), spoken by the centurion, gives us the word "satisfaction."[15] Christ, as both "priest" and sacrificial "victim," releases us from Satan's hell and makes both the temple, and the system of ritual sacrifices, redundant.

Julian's vision of the lacerations, the slashed flesh, and the hot blood did not leave her traumatized, like some who attended Gibson's sadomasochistic "showing." Instead, as the Son went "down with Adam into hell,"[16] something wonderful happened.

> I saw, while looking at the same cross that his blessed expression changed. The changing of his blessed expression changed mine, and I was glad and happy as it was possible to be. Then our Lord made me think happily, 'Where is now one jot of your pain or your sorrow?' And I was very happy. I understood . . . there is no pain on earth, nor in any other place that could hurt us, but everything would cause us joy and bliss.[17]

FERTILITY AND NECESSITY

Medieval religious art often portrays angels catching in chalices the blood that spurts from Christ's side. Sometimes Christ's blood jets out into the mouths of the faithful. There are also representations of the crucifixion as childbirth. These unsavory pictures suggest that the crucified Christ both feeds and gives birth in blood. While they allude to the Eucharistic Mass they also suggest that Christ's flesh does "womanly things."[18]

The New Testament stories of the healing of the women with the hemorrhage and Jairus' daughter (Mark 5:21–43; Luke 8:40–56) are about a lack of fertility.[19] The woman is isolated by her impurity and infertility. The twelve-year-old daughter, the age at which Jewish girls were judged to be nubile, becomes infertile through death. Jesus restores both and

---

15. Richards, "Being delivered from Gibson's hell," 75–80.
16. Julian, *Revelations of Divine Love,* LT.51, 119.
17. Ibid., LT.21, 71–72.
18. Soskice, *The Kindness of God,* 89.
19. Ibid., 93–94.

demonstrates that while impurity has nothing to do with sin, blood has everything to do with fertility.

Ian Bradley in his book *The Power of Sacrifice* argues that giving birth is always a sacrifice. Sacrificing involves a measure of self-limitation.[20] In giving birth to creation God gives freedom to something over and against himself and in so doing sacrifices his own freedom in those areas. He further limits himself by assuming human flesh in the incarnation. These reductions of freedom can be seen as part of a movement towards death. Birth, death, and sacrifice belong together.

Bradley, not unlike Abelard, suggests that the life, teaching, ministry, and death of Jesus demonstrates the remaking power of self-giving-love, however he takes this into another dimension when reflecting on the words "was it not necessary that the Christ should suffer these things, and enter into his glory" (Luke 24:26).

> This overwhelming stress on the inevitability and necessity (of suffering) surely invalidates a portrayal of Jesus' suffering and death simply in terms of a free and voluntary self-sacrifice. Is there not rather a sense here of his submission to the dark and mysterious power of sacrifice, that simultaneously tragic yet life-giving principle at the heart of the cosmos which as the Son of God he is destined to reveal and release?[21]

Death and life, sacrifice and fertility, belong to the very nature of God and are replicated as an aspect of his image in the created order of the earth and the universe.[22] Christ refuses to repudiate the necessity of crucifixion because the cross was rooted in God's very nature before the foundation of the world. Christ "must" suffer to reveal the sacrificial nature of the fertility of God. Even with Christ's death that principle is not removed but has to be pursued by Christians if the image of God is to be restored in humanity. Christians have a vocation—in the words of Charles Wesley—"to make the sacrifice complete".[23]

Sacrifice as power is demonstrated in the cult of the martyrs whose blood was "the seed of the church." It is worth noting that many of those who formulated powerful atonement theories like Irenaeus, Athanasius,

---

20. Bradley, *The Power of Sacrifice*, 68–70.
21. Ibid., 113.
22. Moses, *The Sacrifice of God*, 56.
23. *MHB*, 386.

and Abelard, experienced suffering even to the point of death. Love has restorative power. It does the work of blood.[24]

George Matheson (1842–1906), best remembered for his evocative hymn "O love that wilt not let me go," was a parish minister whose blindness drove him at times to despair. His experience of loneliness and suffering forced him with the inner eyes of faith to meditate upon the sacrificial power of the cross. He came to see that Christ slain from the foundation of the world was the central animating principle of the universe. Like Julian, he realized that fertility comes from the blood of Christ. There is an evolutionary process at work in the ecological mechanisms of the world fed by sacrifice and death. Like Irenaeus and Athanasius, he believed there was a "fall upwards" as the ground "blossoms red" with endless life.[25]

The Victorians, in Matheson's time, emphasized sacrifice. This went hand in hand with social and political radicalism.[26] Intoxicated by evolutionary idealism and economic confidence many theologians believed that God's kingdom could be realized. This inspired many to heroic activity in social reform and mission. Unfortunately the virtue of self-sacrifice became caught up in the patriotism and imperialism of the First World War in which too many young men paid "the supreme sacrifice." As a consequence sacrifice has since become an unpalatable metaphor as "obsolete as the horse drawn plough."[27]

PERSPECTIVES ON SIN, SUFFERING AND SACRIFICE

Julian's reflections on sin—not unlike Abelard's—are very different from Anselm's.

> I believe that it (sin) has no sort of substance or portion of being, nor could it be recognized were it not for the suffering which it causes. And this suffering seems to me to be something transient, for it purges us and makes us know ourselves and pray for mercy.[28]

---

24. Brown, *Cross Talk*, 120.
25. *MHB*, 448.
26. Bradley, *The Power of Sacrifice*, 162–170.
27. Ibid., 5.
28. Julian, *Revelations of Divine Love*, LT.27, 79–81.

Is it true, as Julian maintains, that suffering and sacrifice purge and build up character? Some feminist theologians today have argued against this idea of "soul making" because it ignores the essential tragic character of human existence and the violent cruelty which one human being can inflict on another.[29] It cripples the human spirit and glories in the cult of the victim!

What does Julian mean when she says sin has "no sort of substance"? She explains by telling the story of the Lord and the servant. The servant, sent off by the gentle Lord to fulfill a task, is so delighted that running in haste he falls into a pit and is badly hurt. He falls because of a strong desire to obey his Lord. Even in the pit of pain he is just as eager to do the Lord's bidding as when he first started out. He has not sinned and therefore cannot be blamed. The servant was Christ who is the new Adam.[30]

If sin has no substance then the blood of the crucified has nothing to do with sacrifice and everything to do with grace and joy since "only suffering blames and punishes."[31] Anger in God is an impossibility. Humanity would not exist if God were wrathful. By discarding blame Julian also removes the need for forgiveness.[32]

> And though our earthly mother may allow her child to perish, our heavenly mother Jesus cannot allow us who are his children to perish; for he and none but he is almighty, all wisdom and all love.[33]

HAITI AND NORWICH

Just as Abelard leaves a legacy of love, so Julian leaves us with the hope that 'all shall be well.' The sight a group of survivors standing in the ruins of a church in Port-au-Prince worshipping and pouring out their praises to God is a modern take on those Norwich survivors who, following a consultation with Julian, were filled with gratitude.

Christian discipleship certainly demands self-sacrifice. However in a country like Haiti, where people remain trapped by forces beyond their

---

29. Farley, *Tragic Vision and Divine Compassion*, 53.
30. Julian, *Revelations of Divine Love*, LT.51, 115–119.
31. Ibid., LT.51, 118.
32. Ibid., L.T.49, 112.
33. Ibid., LT.61, 143.

The Wrath of God Satisfied?

control, self-sacrifice has brought no liberation. Although Julian's advice works at a personal level by helping people cope with the harsh realities of life it nevertheless fails because it does not actively confront these realities. As we concluded, when considering Abelard, self-giving-love is not always enough. Something more is needed to combat violent regimes that reduce, demoralize, and destroy. This "something more" is an effective program of organizational help, political restructuring, and re-education. Enter John Calvin!

7

Penal Problems

It was late evening when Fiona Pilkington led he disabled daughter Francecca to her blue Austin Maestro and sat her in it. She fetched their pet rabbit, gave it to her daughter and they set off for a ride to escape the children who roamed their street. This trip was not like any of the others. In the backseat were a pile of clothing and a green ten-litre can of petrol. They drove to a lay-by shielded by trees and parked. It was 11:05pm. The explosion not only tore the car apart but also woke up a shocked nation. The local police had failed to deal with a teenage gang who tormented, taunted, and terrorized a mother and vulnerable daughter. The intimidation had driven then to death.

For ten years Fiona and Francesca had put up with the bullying, the threats, and attacks of the "street kids"—some of whom were as young as ten. In spite of repeated pleas and calls for help from Fiona, her family, and the neighbors, the police had done nothing. No one was arrested, charged, or prosecuted. The gang still runs free even though at least six other families in the street had been intimidated. Fiona, who was depressed, feared for her daughter who had mental age far younger than her years. She could take no more and in September 2009 ended it all.

The news provoked a public outcry. Why didn't the police act? What has happened to law and order? What can be done about gangs of young children who terrify the old and the vulnerable? No one suggested you must love them more; things had gone too far for that. There was an angry desire to punish the miscreants whose empty existence had made them the terror of the street. Interestingly the parents of one of the gang said, "they blame everything on us. Our children are good kids not thugs."

The Wrath of God Satisfied?

Is this what happens with children when all social constraints, both internal and external, are removed? Was this a tragic replay of William Golding's novel the *Lord of the Flies*? Something had gone terribly wrong in that community. Somebody must be accountable. Someone must be blamed and punished; but whom?

THE NEED FOR LAW AND ORDER

One consequence of robbing God of his honour, Anselm believed, was to weaken the social fabric that protected people from the snarling forces of chaos. If women and men are to flourish, honour and/or law must be present. The story of Fiona and Francecca, demonstrates what happens when both are absent.

In chapter 2, I described Luther as someone who blasted a hole in sixteenth-century Europe. Although the structures that propped up medieval society had been tottering for some time, Luther's protest brought the lot down.[1] Pope Leo X called him a "wild boar" who had invaded God's vineyard.[2] The Pope's attempt in 1520 to restrain the rampaging powers came too late. The four horseman of the apocalypse were already galloping across Europe.

By 1533 Christendom was in chaos. Rome was to retaliate with a new Order inspired by Ignatius Loyola. The fanatical radicals of the Reformation were out of control. The Protestant leaders and their successors raged against each other. The secular powers were marshalling their armies. It is at this point that John Calvin makes his appearance to create a system that has subsequently "molded Western Europe and North American culture."[3]

Calvin, like Ignatius Loyola, had studied in the University of Paris. These two giants of the church were to produce rival systems: one centered in Rome sanctioned by the Pope, and the other in Geneva led by a powerful group of lay ministers.[4]

---

1. Whale, *The Protestant Tradition*, 125.
2. Bainton, *Here I Stand*, 114.
3. McGrath, *A Life of John Calvin*, 203.
4. MacCulloch, *Christian History*, 189.

RESTRAINING THE FORCES OF CHAOS

Calvin was a prophet like the Old Testament "watchman" of Ezekiel 33. His two principle objectives were to "proclaim the kingdom of Christ and rid the community of abuses and distortions."[5] Unfortunately he did not have a particularly attractive personality.[6] He has been described as a man unusually sensitive to anxiety, and consequently had an almost pathological fear of confusion and chaos.[7] His diagnosis of the situation was simple. The world was out of joint because God was not honored.[8] Having the "soul of a lawyer," Calvin saw his mission in terms of organizing the world Luther had opened up, and bringing it into conformity with the will of God.[9] His practical program had two ingredients. First he sought to model the ideal Christian community, and second to educate ministers and laity in sound doctrine.

He achieved the first in Geneva, which became the "Mecca of the Protestant Reformation." His successors were to idealize Geneva as "a perfect working model of a godly city run according to the precepts of the Bible."[10]

While Luther had set "gospel" against "law," Calvin unites them. It has been suggested that Calvin comes close to transforming the "gospel" into a new "law."[11] In a context of threat and civil disorder the first requirement is the rule of law to constrain and "force righteousness . . . for the public community of men."[12] Calvin applied this precept, in the city of Geneva, with unremitting zeal. Portraits show him to have an inordinately long nose. His enemies said it was for poking about into other people's affairs.

While his first achievement was Geneva, his second was the *Institutes of the Christian Religion*. The great theme of the *Institutes* is to restore glory to God alone.[13] As a humanist Calvin had a high regard for

5. Ganoczy, *The Young Calvin*, 228.
6. McGrath, *A Life of John Calvin*, 17.
7. Bouwsma, *John Calvin*, 32–34.
8. *Inst*, I.xii.1.
9. Cottret, *Calvin*, 20–22.
10. Gascoine, *The Christians*, 165.
11. Whale, *The Protestant Tradition*, 164.
12. *Inst.* II.vii.10.
13. Ganoczy, *The Young Calvin*, 188.

knowledge and education. It should therefore come as no surprise that the *Institutes* begin with the words: "Nearly all the wisdom we possess, that is to say, true and sound wisdom, consists of two parts: the knowledge of God and of ourselves."[14]

Unfortunately: "Human beings have smothered and corrupted the knowledge of God through ignorance and malice."[15] Becoming fools, human beings have fallen into superstition and confusion.[16] Lost in a labyrinth, the human race exists under the wrath of God.

REVELATION, LAW AND SUBSTITUTION

Following the theological method of Anselm rather than Abelard, Calvin held that reverence and belief are the only gateways to understanding yet unlike his eleventh-century forbearer, Calvin's sole focus of faith is the Scriptures, "wherein lies the Word of God."[17] Because Jesus Christ is the fulfillment of the Law and the Prophets, Old Testament Law is pregnant with promise, acting as a school master to prepare the way for the gospel.[18] It also serves as a mirror to reveal sin in both believers and unbelievers.

Luther coined metaphors from the battlefield, Anselm did his thinking in the context of the feudal system, Abelard within a culture of courtly love, and Julian reflected on the blood of Christ in a time of national disaster. Calvin expounds atonement within a legal framework, drawing on the teaching of Tertullian and Anselm. He therefore works with the metaphors of punishment, satisfaction, substitution, and the payment of debt. Christ's death is the price of our redemption.[19] His sacrifice has the power of "expiating, appeasing and making satisfaction."[20]

Christ's trial before Pilate gives Calvin the opportunity to demonstrate how Christ is both guilty and innocent. At the divine judgment seat, all are pronounced guilty, but Christ "stands in" as our substitute and allows himself to be condemned in our place.

14. *Inst.* I.i.1.
15. *Inst.* I.iv.1.
16. *Inst.* I.iv.12.
17. McGrath, *A Life of John Calvin*, 132.
18. *Inst.* II.vii.2.
19. *Inst.* II.xvii.5.
20. Moses, *The Sacrifice of God*, 133.

> When we hear that Christ was led from the judge's seat to death, and hanged between thieves ... he was reckoned among the transgressors. He suffered death not because of innocence but because of sin ... Thus we shall behold the person of a sinner and evildoer represented in Christ, yet from his shining innocence it will at the same time be obvious that he was burdened with another's sin rather than his own ... We must, above all, remember this substitution, lest we tremble and remain anxious throughout life.[21]

Like Anselm, Calvin insists that the Son was not forced by the Father to die (the charge of "divine child abuse"). Christ chose to empty himself, follow the path of obedience and lay down his life for his friends. Calvin gives this an Abelardian twist by explaining that what "satisfied" God was not Christ's death but his *obedience*.[22] Christ comes as the new Adam.

> Man, who by his disobedience had become lost, should by way of remedy counter it with obedience, satisfy God's judgment, and pay the penalties for sin. Accordingly, our Lord came forth as true man and took the person and the name of Adam in order to take Adam's place in obeying the Father, to present our flesh as the price of satisfaction to God's righteous judgment, and in the same flesh, to pay the penalty that we had deserved.[23]

It would seem that the "presentation of our flesh" and the "payment of the penalty" are not the primary purposes of the incarnation but rather the secondary effects of Christ's obedience. Calvin is returning to the teaching of Paul and Irenaeus.[24] Christ relives the history of Adam yet sanctifies it at each step by reversing Adam's disobedience with his own obedience—so fulfilling God's righteousness.

> Now someone asks how has Christ abolished sin, banished the separation between us and God, and acquired righteousness to render God favorable and kindly towards us? To this we can in general reply that he has achieved this for us by the whole course of his obedience. This is proved by Paul's testimony: 'As by one man's disobedience many were made sinners, so by one man's obedience we are made righteous.'[25]

21. *Inst.* II.xvi.5.
22. Blocher, "The Atonement in John Calvin's Theology," 294.
23. *Inst.* II.xii.3.
24. Brunner, *The Mediator*, 250.
25. *Inst.* II.xvi.5.

CONDEMNATION, PUNISHMENT AND VIOLENCE

One should not be surprised by the similarities between Anselm and Calvin. Both wish to protect society from lawless violence. What is missing, however, from Anselm, but present in Calvin and his successors, is the emphasis on punishment.[26] Calvin resorts to forensic terminology because he believes the greatest threat to our existence comes from the wrath of God.[27] In terrible words, which reflect his own anxiety about the vengeance of God, he describes the experience of the sinner:

> He must anxiously seek ways and means to appease God—and this demands satisfaction. No common assurance is required, for God's wrath and curse always lie upon sinners until they are absolved of guilt. Since he is the righteous Judge, he does not allow his law to be broken without punishment, but is equipped to avenge it.[28]

Calvin, by setting atonement within the context of a criminal court-of-law, traps himself in a system of "retributive" justice. Some of his successors have eagerly developed this "forensic" theology.

Charles Hodge (1797–1878), who taught at Princeton Seminary for fifty years, prioritizes the penal substitution understanding of atonement. Christ's death was not the consequence of an obedient life committed to securing victory over evil. From the beginning God orchestrated his suffering and death. "He was smitten of God and afflicted." There could be no pardon except on the "ground of a forensic penal satisfaction."[29] Hodge argues that Jesus was made the focus of God's wrath so as to satisfy the demands of the law. Hodge reads everything through the lens of criminal justice. His development of Calvinism produces a doctrinal result that is more violent and less humane than Calvin's. Green and Baker's criticism is devastating: "Hodge presents a God who wants to be in relationship with us but is forced to deal with a problem of legal bookkeeping that blocks that relationship. The solution is having God the Father punish the Son."[30]

---

26. Sykes, *The Story of Atonement*, 52.
27. Bouwsma, *John Calvin*, 42.
28. *Inst.* II.xvi.1.
29. McGrath, *A Life of John Calvin*, 211.
30. Green and Baker, *Recovering the Scandal*, 147.

Hodge is quite clear that a just God must inflict punishment. His approach strengthens systems that legitimize retribution. Penal substitution bequeaths a violent legacy to this very day. Stuart Murray argues that this view of atonement fits comfortably into the model of Christendom which has dominated Europe since the fourth century and been exported by mission and conquest throughout the world. Christendom, he argues, offered good news to the poor but ensured that power always remained in the hands of the rich. By embracing patriarchy, hierarchy, and violence, it avoided awkward questions about institutional corruption and systemic injustice. It also fed "just war" theories. Now with the unraveling of Christendom all of these features are being questioned.[31]

It is no accident that the United States, which claims to be the most active Christian nation in the West, has a crusading-gun-culture. George Bush, his right-wing hawks and his evangelical supporters, operated with Christendom assumptions as they sought to exact retributive punishment on Muslims whom they held responsible for 9/11.[32] A retributive doctrine of the cross links fundamentalist Christianity with right-wing politics.[33]

Jeffery, Overy, and Sachs, in their 2007 book *Pierced for our Transgressions*, attempt to present the case for penal substitution from Scripture and tradition. They argue that "wrath pervades Scripture."[34] Their historical survey is selective—though strangely they omit Tertullian, Anselm, and Hodge from their list of the proponents of penal substitution. Their exposition, however, seems more of an imposition upon Scripture. They would not accept my assumption that atonement theories are contextual and utilitarian. Penal substitution for them is the focusing point for all other theories.[35]

THE WRATH OF GOD

Does the wrath of God disappear if we move away from the law-court context and abandon forensic language? C. H. Dodd, a New Testament scholar who influenced a past generation of ministers in England,

---

31. Murray, "Rethinking Atonement," 30–33.
32. Northcott, "Atonement, Violence, and Modern Imperial Order," 94.
33. Fraser, "The Easter of Hawks, Doves," 18.
34. Jeffery, Overy and Sach, *Pierced for our Transgression*, 123.
35. Ibid., 210–220.

interpreted God's wrath in terms of "cause and effect."[36] If I jump from a building I damage myself through the law of gravity. When I sin, I reap the negative consequences of the universal moral law. Today we would have to modify his cause and effect theory since we live in an interconnected world in which all lives are intrinsically bound together. Issues of global injustice and the growing gap between rich and poor suggest very complex global interactions of cause and effect. Others can suffer from the consequences of my sin, while my sin may have little or no effect on me. Dodd's explanation, arising from his own exposition of Romans 1:18, is unsatisfactory as is his insistence that *hilastēron* has nothing to do with propitiation.[37]

Paul makes it clear in Romans 1:18 that wrath cannot be detached from God. It is not a mechanistic process but rather a divine act of personally trashing human idolatry. God's wrath underscores how seriously he views sin because sin, when unrestrained, leads to civil disorder and social disintegration. "Wrath" always remains the "wrath of God," because God chooses "to give us up" (Rom 1:24, 26) to follow the path we have chosen even though it leads to our destruction.[38] Our sinful actions do not invite God's wrath, but rather prove that God's wrath is already active. Miroslav Volf—the Croatian theologian—comes to this conclusion from his own experiences of the 1990s Balkans conflict.

> I used to think that wrath was unworthy of God. Isn't God love? Shouldn't divine love be beyond wrath? God is love, and God loves every person and every creature. That's exactly why God is wrathful against some of them. My last resistance to the idea of God's wrath was as a casualty of war in the former Yugoslavia, the region from which I come. According to some estimates, 200,000 people were killed and over 3,000,000 were displaced. My villages and cities were destroyed, *my* people shelled day in and day out, some of them brutalized beyond imagination, and I could not imagine God not being angry. Or think of Rwanda in the last decade of the past century where 800,000 people were hacked to death in one hundred days. How does God react to such carnage? By doting on the perpetrators in a grandparently fashion? By refusing to condemn the bloodbath? . . . Though I used to complain about the indecency of the idea of God's wrath, I came to think that I would

---

36. Dodd, *Letter to the Romans*, 22–24.
37. Jeffery, Overy and Sach, 83–89; Dodd, *Romans*, 55.
38. Cranfield, *Romans*, 120.

have to rebel against a God who *wasn't* wrathful at the sight of the world's evil. God isn't wrathful in spite of being love. God is wrathful *because* God is love.[39]

CALVIN'S LEGAL LEGACY

While it may seem a good idea to remove forensic ideas from atonement, a disturbing feature of our age is the way in which an ever-increasing number of people are resorting to litigation. The threat of "law" increasingly dominates our lives. While we may accept that laws are historically and socially conditioned, when wrath is separated from love legalism threatens so that both "wrath" and "law" become tyrannical.[40] Nevertheless, as Calvin recognized, "law" has a vital part to play in preserving community. The practical application of law protects vulnerable people like Fiona Pilkington and her daughter Francesca.

Although many Christians would wish to dissociate God from acts of violence, the Bible does not do so. The prevalent message of the Old Testament is that human suffering arises from human sinfulness.[41] Again and again God is introduced within this consequential link (2 Kgs 22:13; 2 Chr 28:1; Job 19:11, 42:7; Isa 10:6, 13:9; Lam 2:2; Ezek 22:31; Hos 13:11; Nah 1:1; Hab 3:8; Zeph 1:15, 2:13). A quick examination of these texts reveals God's wrath to be directed more against Israel than against the other nations. To delete divine wrath from God's relationship with his covenant people would remove their distinctiveness. "The refusal to use coercions and to inflict harm or damage is really a refusal to enforce boundaries."[42] It would also prevent them from being the amazing people that God intends them to be.[43] Because divine punishment was God's attempt to get Israel to return to their covenantal vocation, I suggest that the Exile is more about restorative justice than retributive justice.

Calvin had a vision of a community of righteousness and love. This could be achieved if God's glory and honor were safeguarded. How are we to interpret this in a contemporary context of violence, criminality, and

39. Volf, *Free of Charge*, 138.
40. Watson, *Let God be God*, 124.
41. Thompson, *Where is the God of Justice?*, 175.
42. Boersma, *Violence, Hospitality, and the Cross*, 61.
43. Thompson, *Where is the God of Justice?*, 98.

The Wrath of God Satisfied?

debt? This question takes us into part 2, which begins with a theological diagnosis of violence, and leads to an exploration of the nature of God. We shall not only see that divine wrath is a shadow cast by the blinding light of love, but also that it is an essential ingredient, within God's purpose in Christ, for establishing a just world.

PART TWO

Wrath Satisfied?

8

A Wheel of Fire

THE HEAVY RAIN WAS unabating. Everywhere the fields were saturated and our coach sometimes ploughed through the water that swamped the sides of the road. Our small party had come prepared with waterproofs and umbrellas. All of us were pensive as we journeyed from Krakow to Auschwitz. I kept remembering the images of the "thinking Christ" we had seen in the churchyard at Zakopane—a picturesque resort in the Tatra Mountains. This Christ held his head in his hands, and his expression seemed to say, "What have you done to my world?" On our tour of Auschwitz and Birkenau we were to witness the dark side of human achievement.

It was not just the cynical disregard for human life that disturbed me. The twentieth century has a history of unspeakable violence, mass murder, and torture. What I personally found appalling was the cold-blooded search for efficiency in exterminating 1.3 million men, women, and children.

Our party tramped for two hours around Auschwitz, going from hut to hut, and finally ending up in the gas chamber and adjacent crematorium. For a brief moment I was able to stand alone in this vortex of evil. The rain pattered down through holes in the roof through which lethal cyclone B gas was released to kill several hundred people stacked like cattle in a stall of death. It took twenty minutes for them to die. Now only rain came through the holes. God was shedding tears.

This chapter sets atonement in the context of war crimes, murder, and ethnic cleansing. Every one of us, through our action or inaction, contributes to this violent legacy of death. Giles Fraser acknowledges that in his darker moments he is ashamed to be a Christian.

> The fact that the crucifixion has been the basis for centuries of anti-Semitic propaganda must remind all Christians of their own capacity for violence and brutality.[1]

Looking at the example of Dr. Jekyll and Mr. Hyde, he suggests that the latter can only operate in the dark because these are unexamined spaces brought about by Dr. Jekyll's pious avoidance of his own darker motivation. They are not two people but one. Western Christians, the product of democratic liberalism, identify with victims but leave their own potential for violence and hatred intact. "The idea that we might catch a glimpse of our own reflection in the face of a Nazi guard is a terrifying thought."[2] We therefore protect ourselves from our own capacity for violence by describing evil as something alien and foreign to us.

RENÉ GIRARD, SACRIFICE, AND VIOLENCE

For Julian, sin has no substance. For Abelard, sin is a disfunctionality that creates an obstruction without ultimately negating the good. Anselm has a more somber assessment. Sin has an objective reality. If it is not destroyed, it will destroy. Calvin, following Anselm, believes sin to be the root of lawlessness, corruption, and malice, enslaving both the powerful and the powerless in a self-perpetuating cycle of wrath. René Girard (b.1923)—French historian, literary critic, and philosopher—explores this from an anthropological point of view.[3]

He argues that violence arises when humans compete and imitate each other in their pursuit of a single goal. Mutual rivalry can become so intense and contagious, that it leads to murder. Violence had its beginning in Cain (Gen 4:1–5).

The Hebrew word for Cain means "bring forth." Cain, the firstborn son, inherited productive land. The Hebrew for Abel means "nothing" or "vapor." The two did not start equal. Cain had fertile land; Abel did not and became a wandering nomad. Their wish to offer God the best

---

1. Fraser, "The Easter of Hawks, Doves, Victims and Victimisers," 12.
2. Ibid., 14.
3. Girard, *I see Satan Fall like Lightening*, 24.

sacrifice drove them to compete. When they brought their gifts, God took Abel's side—the side of the disadvantaged. This provoked an explosive reaction in Cain. He enticed Abel into the field and like a wild beast killed him (Gen 4:6–8). Cain according to Girard was the first murderer and the founder of the urban culture of violence (Gen 4:17). Violence is mimetic—it imitates itself.[4]

Why doesn't violence escalate to such a level that human beings destroy themselves? Girard explains that we re-direct our anger onto victims who become scapegoats chosen because they are different. The Jews have always been picked on. In the Middle Ages when panics occurred, lepers, foreigners, wise women, and the disabled were targeted.

> Communities mimetically transferred all their hostilities to the single victim and become reconciled the basis of the resulting illusion.[5]

Pilate and Herod became friends on the day of Christ's crucifixion (Luke 23:12). Pilate also understood that the crowd would not be pacified without a victim and therefore sacrifices Jesus to prevent further public disorder.

Girard could have used the story of Jonah as an example of anti-Semitism, but instead interprets it as an example of "scapegoating." The ship is the community. Lots are cast. Jonah is hurled into the sea. The sailors offer a sacrifice. This leads Girard to investigate other sacrificial rituals.

> Bloody sacrifices are attempts to repress or moderate the internal conflicts of primitive or archaic communities, and they do this by reproducing as exactly as possible, at the expense of the victims substituted for the original victim, a real act of violence.[6]

These primal ideas of "substitution" and "sacrifice" are present in atonement theories. Girard suggests that a ritual blood sacrifice is an agreed act of violence to end violence. Although the metaphor of sacrifice may be unpalatable today, the smoking crematoria of Auschwitz and the 1994 bloodbath in Rwanda[7] are savage reminders that powerful elites

---

4. Ibid., 19.
5. Daniels, "Passing the Peace," 131.
6. Ibid., 78.
7. Grey, *To Rwanda and Back*.

maintain their hold by creating victims. The bloody killings, burnings, and destruction of those judged to be different is a sub-text of human history serving to renew the social cohesion of the group that regards itself as superior. The Balkans conflict is a case in point.

REVELATION AS A ROAD TO LIBERATION

The dragon, the devil, and all dark forces are personified in Satan, within Girard's exposition. Satan keeps the wheels of violence spinning. He sustains himself as a parasite imitating God in a perverse and confusing manner.[8] He persuades us that "good" violence is the answer to "bad violence." The US and UK Governments assumed this when invading Iraq.[9] Mimetic imitation flourishes because it is not understood by the participants.[10] Girard says Jesus died not to appease God's wrath but to break the repetitive cycle of violence by revealing its essential nature. In the cross violence is seen to be human violence.[11]

> By depriving the victim mechanism of the darkness that must conceal it so it can continue to control human culture, the Cross shakes up the world . . . Satan is no longer able to limit his capacity for destruction. Satan will destroy his kingdom, and he will destroy himself.[12]

Peter Schmiechen,[13] in his chapter on Christ the Reconciler, analyses the breakdown of relationships within the Corinthian Church. Division arose because some claimed to have superior wisdom and spiritual power. Paul responds by reminding them that, on the cross, God reveals the world's wisdom to be folly and its power emptiness.[14] The first step to liberation from the "powers" which hold us in captivity is to unmask

---

8. Girard, *I see Satan Fall like Lightening*, 44.
9. Reed, *Just War?*, 104–108.
10. Girard, *I see Satan Fall like Lightening*, 126.
11. Boersma, *Violence, Hospitality, and the Cross*, 139.
12. Girard, *I see Satan Fall like Lightening*, 142.
13. Schmiechen, *Saving Power*, 272.
14. Ibid., 275.

them.[15] Christ's death on the cross publically demonstrates that Satan is an impostor (Col 2:14–15).[16]

The Liberation Theologians working amongst the poor in Latin America realized that Anselm's classic way of approaching theology as a movement from "faith" to "understanding" did not deliver freedom. They therefore started, as Abelard did, with reason and understanding. "Faith is the second act".[17] The "powers" which trap people in poverty can be unmasked through investigating and analyzing the structural, economic, and political forces at work in a particular context. The theologians also recognized that the poor had become passive because the picture of Christ presented to them, by their conquerors, was that of "the conquered one." The poor, by embracing the tortured Christ, live in a "long and bloody Good Friday" and put their faith in someone who sanctions their powerlessness.[18]

How are victims to secure their liberation? Without the resources of military force, economic power, and affluence, the underprivileged must resort to trickery.[19] The non-violent direct action against Pharaoh's program of ethnic-cleansing, conducted by the Jewish midwives of Exodus 1, took control away from the ruling elite. This forces them to use an even greater measure of violence which ultimately undermines their moral credibility—as is happening within President Bashar Al-Assad's Syria. By interpreting the death of Jesus through the lens of strategic cunning—as Gregory of Nyssa does—we arrive at the conclusion that Jesus did not come to abolish evil, but rather to show us how to resist it.

RECONCILIATION AND EXCHANGE

The word "reconciliation" comes from the Latin, *re-* "again", *con-* "with" and *sella-*"seat." It is the action of again sitting and eating together at the same table. This is not the cozy fellowship of friends drinking tea together; it is the sitting and eating with your enemy. In the Old Testament stories of Cain and Abel, Jacob and Esau, and the New Testament parable of the

15. Ibid., 282.
16. Ibid., 138.
17. Brown, *Liberation Theology*, 55.
18. Ray, *Deceiving the Devil*, 77–78.
19. Ibid., 124, 138, 141.

two sons (Luke 15), one party refuses to share a meal with the other. Cain, Esau, and the elder brother decide to stay outside in the field.

The Greek verb "to reconcile" is *katallassein*. The root—*allassein* ("to exchange") is derived from *allos* ("other"). The whole word suggests the action of not only sitting together but of putting oneself in the place of the other.

> Reconciliation begins to become a reality when, without surrendering our identity, who we are, but opening up ourselves to the 'other,' we enter into the space between, exchanging places with the other in a conversation which takes us beyond ourselves.[20]

While Tertullian, Anselm, and Calvin thought of "satisfaction" in terms of debt, compensation and punishment, the "satisfaction" required by the *Truth and Reconciliation Commission* of South Africa was to hear the truth declared by both the recipients and the perpetrators of violence. They had to sit together in the same public space and give an honest account of their activities so that, through an exchange of stories, each would come to identify with "the other".[21]

Miroslav Volf argues that only forgiveness can break the power of the remembered past and transcend it.[22] Forgiveness takes control away from the oppressor and gives power back to the victim who can then release the oppressor. Unfortunately, anger burns deeply in the heart of every victim who may also be paralyzed by shame. If the perpetrator is repentant, then forgiveness comes more easily. This seldom happens. A "saintly" or "surface" response of forgiveness may also be unhelpful because it lets the perpetrator off-the-hook. Both victor and victim are locked in a wheel of mutual exclusion, unable to forgive, and unable to repent.[23]

The saying "we must forgive and forget" is also unhelpful. On one of the prison walls in Auschwitz is the statement: "If we forget history, history repeats itself." A new future only opens up when both parties "remember correctly." If we forget, we learn nothing and the terrors of the past repeat themselves. If we do not forget, then the pain of the past blights the present. Volf says that the healing of memories will not take place until both parties "receive the 'grace of non-remembering.'"[24] He

20. De Gruchy, *Reconciliation*, 153.
21. Ibid., 160.
22. Volf, *Exclusion and Embrace*, 116–118.
23. Ibid., 120.
24. Ibid., 138.

also recognizes that the process of reconciliation will only be complete beyond the grave. "If heaven cannot rectify Auschwitz, then the memory of Auschwitz must undo the experience of heaven."[25]

RECONCILIATION AND JUSTICE

Victim and victor are bound together on a wheel of fire. Hitler's murderous enterprise had a twofold effect. It accelerated the concern for victims while at the same time it demoralized them.[26] According to Girard, the church's concern for victims has now become hysterical. Both oppressors and victims are under judgment. The oppressors and the rich, with their sins of self-justification and arrogance, trample and oppress the poor. The victims and the powerless often use their victimhood as an excuse. They have their own sins of envy and hate. Reciprocity will only be achieved through self-sacrificial acts performed by both parties.[27]

Although truth is a foundational ingredient in reconciliation, truth is inseparable from justice. Girard omits justice from his exposition of the cross. This may be because the idea of universal justice has been attacked by post-modernists who find it inherently oppressive—certainly some terrible injustices have been committed in the name of "justice." Although some use the word "justice" to justify their own actions it is not a utilitarian word, we must therefore take is very seriously.[28]

Justice is a powerful ingredient in Paul's understanding of atonement. His use of the word "justification" (*dikaiōsis*) springs from his belief that God himself is righteous (*dikaios*). Justification belongs to the process of reconciliation.[29] Kenneth Grayston—one-time Professor of Theology in the University of Bristol[30]—explained justification in this way.

Paul did not meet the "resurrected Christ" on the Damascus Road but rather the "glorified Christ" who was Paul's eschatological judge. Paul in effect faced the last judgment before the "end of the ages." He was not

---

25. Ibid., 136.
26. Girard, *I see Satan Fall like Lightening*, 176.
27. Ibid., 146.
28. Volf, *Exclusion and Embrace*, 220–227.
29. Cranfield, *Commentary on the Epistle to the Romans*, 256.
30. These insights came from an interchange with a group of minister following a lecture by Prof. Grayston, at Ammerdown, near Bristol, UK in May 1979.

acquitted but rather pronounced guilty of crucifying Christ present within the church. Paul, the oppressor, was not pardoned or declared righteous, but instead sentenced to a lifetime of penal servitude. He now becomes "the slave of Jesus Christ." Through his "service" he would be shown "how much he must suffer" for the sake of Christ's name (Acts 9:16). Paul would henceforth be part of that apostolic company chosen to complete "what is lacking in Christ's afflictions for the sake of the body, that is the church" (Col 1:24). The theological implications for justification are far-reaching. Paul is no longer the slave of sin but has a new master in whose service is perfect freedom. Most important of all, he will not have to face the last judgment because he has already faced it. He is therefore free of the fear of it and has peace. There is no condemnation because the last judgment is behind him. This becomes true for all who are "in Christ" (Rom 8:1). The Christ, who will meet him in the future, will not condemn (Phil 3:10–11) but instead assess the work he has done, and reward him accordingly (1 Cor 3:13–15).

In the Damascus Road story, Ananias, who can be regarded as the representative target of Paul's reign of terror, becomes the instrument of Paul's release (Acts 9.10–15). By risking all, Ananias achieves reconciliation between the oppressor and the oppressed. Paul, the former persecutor, spends the rest of his days making restitution. He does so joyfully because he regards his service neither as demand nor as an attempt to avoid punishment, but rather as a creative opportunity to work with God rather than against him.

RECONCILIATION AND REDEMPTION

While the New Testament understands redemption as a release from slavery to sin, Anselm interpreted redemption as a release from indebtedness. His insight has a contemporary ring.

Originally in the Old Testament the word 'debt' (variations on the (Greek word *opheilein*—"to owe") lay within the sphere of "covenant law." Every seven years debts had to be remitted by the creditor (Deut 15:2), and in the Jubilee year the slate was wiped clean. This understanding changed during the Inter-Testamental period. Sin, within the covenant relationship, began to be understood not just as disobedience but also as an outstanding debt. Therefore we find Jesus, according to Matthew, instructing us to ask God to "forgive us our debts (*opheiléma*) as we forgive our debtors" (Matt 6:12).

Peter Selby in his book *Grace and Mortgage,* reflecting on the global debt crisis, unmasks the falsehoods that underpin contemporary economic systems.[31] The gospel message about God removing debt is not necessarily good news because human beings are trapped in a cycle of credit and debt. This subjects everyone to the power of money—"a subjugation experienced not only by the victims of chronic indebtedness but also by the world's creditor nations."[32] In an economy of monetary exchange, those receiving a gift to lift them from debt come to regard it as a "hand-out." This undermines their dignity and responsibility.

In Matthew's parable of the laborers in the vineyard (Matt 20:1–16) those who worked the hardest grumbled bitterly about those who had worked for only one hour. Handouts polarize the "haves" and the "have-nots." The Gospel comment about the last being first and the first last is not, says Selby, a legislative utterance ushering in some new rules for an economy of exchange. It is about a gift economy confronting the economy of exchange.[33] Anselm had argued similarly. Covenantal thinking must replace contractual thinking.

NOT THE SUM-TOTAL OF RECONCILIATION.

Girard does not address the question 'is the wrath of God satisfied?' He eliminates it. Wrath is a human mechanism driving the wheel of fire. That wheel will never stop spinning until reconciliation is worked out practicably from within a covenantal and theological understanding. What has been missing in this chapter—apart from our brief consideration of Paul's experience on the Damascus Road—is humanity's need to be reconciled to God. This is minimized in Girard and the Liberation theologians. Without the God dimension, human acts of reconciliation, though beneficial, will not touch the roots of our being.

The apostle Paul, in his exposition of "justification" in Romans 3:25–26, argues that the righteousness of God has to be set out in two senses: "to prove (i.e. show) at this present time that he (God) himself

31. Selby, *Grace and Mortgage.*
32. Ibid., 157.
33. Ibid., 151.

is righteous and (second) that he justifies him who has faith in Jesus."[34] Sin's consequences are so disastrous that a simple act of forgiveness would compromise God's righteousness. Thus if the holy God is to forgive, he must at the same time do it in such a way as to show that he remains a just and righteous God. Paul recognizes that God must both *be* righteous, and be *seen* to be righteous.[35]

P. T. Forsyth argued that in a genuine reconciliation between persons, change takes place in both parties. Since God is the prime mover in the process of reconciliation, his action not only changes humanity but God changes himself.[36] In Old Testament language, "his anger is turned aside." The atonement is not about Christ enabling God to forgive by adjusting the balance between justice and mercy. This resorts to the type of legal book-keeping we encountered with Hodge in our last chapter. Forsyth, in setting forth a God of holy love, argues that justice and mercy are one of the same. If we human beings are to establish a more enduring reconciliation between communities and persons then we must also be reconciled to God. In addition God has to be reconciled to us. Furthermore, as we shall see in the next two chapters, God has to be reconciled to himself!

---

34. Forsyth, *Justification of God*, 174.
35. Cranfield, *Commentary on the Epistle to the Romans*, 213.
36. Forsyth, *The Work of Christ*, 75–76.

9

There Is No God

A FEW DAYS BEFORE the eleventh of September 2010, Pastor Terry Jones a former hotel manager and born again Christian sat in his dingy office in Gainesville, Florida, and announced his "international burn a Koran day" to commemorated 9/11. Thousands of Afghans took to the streets chanting "Death to America." A demonstrator was killed. Muslims around the world raged. General Petraeus, in Afghanistan, spoke of the increased risk posed to US troops. While politicians in Washington fumed, Pastor Jones, who had never met a Muslim in his life, seemed unaware that he had lit a global bonfire of hate. Although he was eventually pressured to postpone his action, the damage had been done. The image of bigoted American religion had been disseminated by phone and web across the world.

Religion can be fanatical. Richard Dawkins and Christopher Hitchens[1] have been saying this for some time. There is no denying that religion can be a force for evil, but it can also be a force for good. Keith Ward, in his book, *Is Religion Dangerous*, concludes that it is human beings, whether religious or not, who are dangerous.[2]

Karl Barth says religion can be a form of unbelief.[3] The character of any religion relates to its conception of God. Traditional representations of God as omnipotent, omniscient, omnipresent, and masculine, can not only distort our understanding of atonement but "screw up" people's lives.

---

1. Hitchens, *God is Not Great*.
2. Ward, *Is Religion Dangerous?*, 39.
3. CD 1/2:303.

The Wrath of God Satisfied?

One traumatized survivor of child sexual abuse commented, "I had to be careful because He saw everything. I didn't understand His almightiness, because he didn't intervene and left me to fend for myself."[4]

Not only do metaphysical categories blight the theology of God, but also the philosophical God of theism can be equally problematic. When the Christian religion is shaped by such divinities it is inevitable that unacceptable interpretations of satisfaction, punishment, and blood, warp atonement theology.

Using labels to explain God produces false gods. Thomas Aquinas, realizing this, defined God by what he is not. The result was sixty volumes of theology. Should the word "God" be discarded altogether?[5] The slogan, *There Is No God*—which appeared on some London buses in 2009—may not be as negative as some might suppose. The first Christians were called "atheists" because they would not offer worship to the "gods" of this world. "God" is not an object to be examined or dissected. God is "subject" yet beyond subjects. "God" should be regarded, grammatically, as a verb rather than as a noun.[6] God is mystery and—as we observed in chapter 1—he has chosen a scandalous form of revelation to detonate all of our ideas, philosophies, projections, explanations, descriptions, and fantasies of divinity.

THE PUZZLE OF PREDESTINATION

The context for experiencing the mystery of God is worship. Rowan Williams says,

> When we enter a Church to worship we must be mindful of our fractured awareness. Although we may not wish to endorse all the words and content of worship, we must 'ask ourselves what we are taught about the strangeness and sometimes the terror of the Word of God.'[7]

This is particularly so when we encounter references to predestination as we did in connection with Abelard, Julian, and Calvin. In the

---

4. Ray, *Deceiving the Devil*, 45.
5. Soskice, *The Kindness of God*, 13.
6. Ibid., 14.
7. Williams, *Open to Judgement*, 116.

There Is No God

coronation anthem of Ephesians, there are some references to election and predestination.

> He chose us in Christ before the foundation of the world (1:4).
> He destined us . . . according to the good pleasure of his will (1:5).

God's decision to elect certain individuals and one particular nation, dominates the Old Testament. Ephesians re-invents election by placing Christ at the centre to enable a process of re-creation to trickle through history.[8]

We have already come across *anakephalaiōsis* (1:10) when considering Irenaeus. The word translated "recapitulation," can be interpreted as "re-harmonization." This takes us into the concert hall. Since the fall of Adam, the dissonant cries of the victims of violence can be likened to the sounds an orchestra makes before the performance of a great symphony. Christ, who created the symphony in the first place, steps onto the stage of history as the conductor. His task is to inspire the orchestra to produce music of such quality, that all members of the audience want to become performers. That's how Ephesians understands election and predestination. It is a movement from the one, to the some, to the many, to all. Election's scope is primal and universal. Christians are chosen, as God's active musicians, to communicate the sound of a planet "re-tuned" to God's music.

Calvinists, like Hodge, set predestination at the beginning of their theological systems.[9] Calvin did not. He began his *Institutes* with the Trinity. Predestination does not make its appearance until book III—after his exposition of justification by faith. It is introduced here as an incentive for faith and good works.[10] Predestination, in Calvin's preaching and pastoral practice was more peripheral than some later Calvinists might have wished.

THE WONDER OF THE TRINITY

Augustine (354–430) gave the Western Church a strong interpretation of predestination. He also provided the church with a mature expression of

---

8. Stuckey, *Into the Far Country*, 53–56.
9. Blocher, "The Atonement in John Calvin's Theology," 294.
10. Wendel, *Calvin*, 264–66.

Trinity.[11] In chapter 4, I marveled at Anselm's "wrap-around" Trinity, the lack of hierarchical relationship between Father, Son, and Spirit and the interaction of persons sharing a common life without blending or disconnection. This he inherited from Augustine. The focus was not on God the Father, but instead upon the divine substance labeled "essence."[12] Emphasis is therefore placed on the "oneness," or the unity, of God. Father, Son, and Spirit are not separate individuals but persons in a mutual relationship, operating with a single will and purpose. The charge of divine child abuse stands only if Father and Son have an independent existence. In the "wrap-around" Trinity of Augustine and Anselm it is impossible for one person to inflict pain on another without suffering that same pain within himself.

The theologians of the Eastern Church coined the word *perichoresis* to describe a similar "wrap-around" Trinity. The word means "to proceed about each other." It suggests a sort of dynamic "hoe-down" taking place within God—a finding and losing, a circling and spiraling of partners. Within the eternal life of the Trinity an "exchange of energies" is taking place.[13] The persons of the Trinity "do not merely exist and live in one another, they also bring one another mutually to manifestation in divine glory."[14] If glory within the Trinity is an exchange of life and energy, then in atonement theology this translates into, what Luther describes as, a "happy exchange" between Christ and us.

While the Trinity, at one level, can be regarded as a formula describing what God is, its real significance is to prohibit what God is not. Trinitarian doctrine subverts hierarchical relationships between Father and Son—which were the "left-overs" of the Athanasius' struggle with Arius. If God is mystery then resorting to a mathematical formula will always fail. We live in a four-dimensional world of time and space, yet scientists tell us that universes of up to ten or eleven dimensions can exist. A three in one formula could be too small!

---

11. Kelly, *Early Christian Doctrines*, 259–260.
12. Ibid., 272.
13. Moltmann, *The Trinity and the Kingdom of God*, 174.
14. Ibid., 176.

GOD THE FATHER AND MOTHER

It is generally assumed that God has a masculine gender. Mary Daly argues that if God is male, then male is God—thus excluding women from salvation.[15] Certainly not all traditional theologians are trapped in male stereotypes. Julian of Norwich spoke of Christ as Mother and Anselm in his devotional material appealed to the female.

One can remove the male monopoly by assigning a female gender to a member of the Trinity; the Holy Spirit is an obvious candidate. The feminine can also be introduced by re-presenting the male Christ as the female *Christa*. On the cross the crucified *Christa* "yells no to the male God."[16] Mary Grey explains that the prologue of John's Gospel is an adaptation of a pagan hymn praising *Sophia*—wisdom. *Sophia*, unlike the male l*ogos*, is female and relational. *Sophia* is the primal depth or womb from which creation is shaped by the *logos*.[17]

Although the word "Father" is used to describe one member of the Trinity, "father" is only used a few times in the Old Testament. God, described as the "God of our fathers," is the verb "I am who I am" (Exod 3:14). In the New Testament Jesus uses "Abba"—the intimate title for Father.

> The God, who is 'not Father' in Exodus, becomes father and spouse in the Prophetic literature and is revealed in the intimacy of the address of 'Abba' in the books of the New Testament.[18]

The Biblical emphasis is not on "maleness" but on relational intimacy as gender issues, within the God "who gave you birth" (Deut 32:18), are overcome. God is not bisexual or transsexual; he/she transcends the gender categories of male and female.

There are therefore gender issues at work in the formulation and in our contemporary perception of the traditional theories of atonement. Many women find the theories unacceptable because of the presence of sadomasochistic elements. As noted in chapter 1, a suffering or tortured women would not have shocked many in times past. Because women have always been victimized by men, demanding brokenness, as an expression of repentance, is more applicable to men than to women. Because women

---

15. Thompson, *Crossing the Divide*, 117.
16. Ibid., 126.
17. Grey, *Outrageous Pursuit of Hope*, 81–85.
18. Soskice, *The Kindness of God*, 77.

are treated as second-class citizens within most worldwide social structures, repentance for women is more about actively engaging in a search for healing, affirmation and friendship.[19] Without pushing the gender differences too far, I am suggesting that if a man is to become a disciple he must sacrifice his desire to control. For a woman to become a disciple, she has to sacrifice and leave behind her sense of unworthiness, since this can be a comfort blanket.

THE PASSION OF GOD

When metaphysical categories crumble, and gender issues are taken into account, a term like *aseity*—describing God's inability to suffer change—is misleading. The word comes from a Stoic background and suggests mastering one's passions. When used theologically, it portrays an indifferent God without *pathos* and without passion. Because suffering involves change, the word was coined to safeguard the eternal changelessness of a God who is the same yesterday, today, and forever.[20] It was inevitably that attempts to square the circle of *pathos* and *aseity* would hit difficulties. Christ suffered, it was suggested, in his human flesh and not in his divine nature. Such a neat separation between the divine and human, as we found in Anselm, fails to explain how human nature can be redeemed.

In a "wrap-around" Trinity, if Christ suffers then the Father also suffers. This line of thinking[21] was ultimately to bear fruit. It is exemplified in the last lines of Charles Wesley's great atonement hymn.

> Never love nor sorrow was
> Like that my Savior showed;
> See him stretched on yonder cross,
> And crushed beneath our load!
> Now discern the Deity,
> Now his heavenly birth declare;
> Faith cries out: 'Tis he, 'tis he,
> My God, that suffers there! [22]

---

19. Thompson, *Crossing the Divide*, 156–158.
20. Moltmann, 220.
21. "Patripassianism" is the teaching that the Father suffered like the Son. It arose in the third century and was regarded as a heresy. The changelessness of the divine nature had to be protected.
22. *MHB*, 191.

There Is No God

The traumas of two World Wars and the horrors of genocide have forced twentieth-century theologians to take this route. Divine pathos, rather than divine indifference, is now the starting point. Studdert Kennedy, who was an army chaplain in the 1914–1918 world war—affectionately known as Woodbine Willy because he distributed cigarettes to the soldiers in the trenches—articulated divine pathos in his "rough rhymes." In a poem entitled "The Sorrow of God," he imagines God suffering on the cross at Calvary and suggests, in a most daring way, that there might be an eternal Calvary of pain and shame. Reflecting on God's coming to earth in Christ and his passion and death, the poem pictures God weeping because of the violence human beings inflict on each other. Although God could give up on us Kennedy tells us that he has chosen instead to suffer with us in an endless Calvary. God is not absent from the shattered limbs and madness of the battlefield but is present within it.[23]

Karl Barth set this in a more scholarly framework by turning the doctrine of predestination on its head, and insisting that God embraces the negative side of divine predestination. Thus God takes human rejection into himself. God becomes the judge, who is judged in our place.

> In his Son He elected Himself as the covenant partner of man . . . he willed to make good this affronting and disturbing of His majesty . . . not by avenging Himself on its author, but by Himself bearing the inevitable wrath and perdition . . . . Predestination means that from all eternity God has determined upon man's acquittal at his own cost . . . the Lamb slain from the foundation of the world.[24]

In Christ, God abandons the "form of God" to come into our "far country." He chooses, as God, to enter into self-limitation.[25] Bonhoeffer, writing from prison in 1944, a few weeks before his execution, gives this Barthian insight a further twist.

> God allows himself be edged out of the world and onto the cross. God is weak and powerless in the world, and that is exactly the way, the only way, in which he can be with us and help us . . . only a suffering God can help.[26]

---

23. Kennedy, "The Sorrow of God."
24. *CD* 2/2:166–169.
25. *CD* 4/1:187–188.
26. Bonhoeffer, *Letters and Papers from Prison*, 164.

The Wrath of God Satisfied?

Jürgen Moltmann, who belonged to the same Lutheran Tradition as Bonhoeffer, having reflected on the horrors of Auschwitz, published his ground breaking book *The Crucified God*. The book centers on Christ's shout of dereliction "My God, my God why have you forsaken me." Moltmann argues that this cry matches the "godforsakenness of all reality."[27] The cross publicly exposes the falseness of theism, atheism, and political ideology.[28]

BLAMING GOD

Augustine traced suffering back to the sin of Adam. Julian also registered this connexion between sin and suffering but puzzles over why God sees no sin in her and refuses to blame or punish.

This created a theological problem for her. The church taught that all sinners live under the judgment of God and deserve his wrath. Julian was no heretic. She therefore acknowledges that she lives with two unresolved revelations. The first, coming from her "showing," assigns no blame. The second revelation, coming from the church, teaches that God does blame. She prays for grace to "understand these two judgments as they apply to me."[29]

If God is indeed righteous who, if not Adam, is accountable for the sufferings of the world? Although one might accuse the devil, Old Testament characters like Jeremiah and Job blame God. Job's words and silences are protests against a destroying God. While his friends are theologically correct in spelling-out orthodox truths, Job realizes that their explanations will not do. Is this because "truth" has to be incarnated into particular historical situations before it can be true revelation?[30] Job is righteous because he continues to express belief in a holy God even in a divine whirlwind of destruction.

God must carry responsibility for the existence of evil because "he is the one who ultimately sets the boundaries in which we live and move and have our being."[31] God limited himself in creating free human beings.

27. Moltmann, *The Crucified God*, 146–150.
28. Bauckham, *Moltmann*, 66, 80.
29. Julian, *Revelations of Divine Love*, LT.46, 107.
30. CD 4/3:454–460.
31. Roth, "A Theodicy of Protest," 11.

There Is No God

What if God's self-restraint was too excessive? In giving up control, did God permit the emergence of the wild and unrestrained?[32]

Karl Barth calls this alien unrestrained reality "nothingness." This stubborn evil element is denied "the benefit of God's preservation, concurrence and rule."[33] "Nothingness" is the shadow side of God's creating. It is not emptiness or void, rather "nothingness" is diabolical because it is without God. "It is the comprehensive negation of the creature and its nature."[34] Its existence is the product of God's "non-willing."

A tragic and destructive process is at work in our world. Wheat and tares have been so chaotically scattered within creation, that evil appears to thrive more rapidly than goodness. God, from our point of view, does not seem to have created "the best of all possible worlds." Studdert Kennedy's line about "the blistering flame of eternal shame" at the heart of God is far more profound than it might seem.

The awesome message of Christianity is that God, because of his graciousness, "freely chooses" to hold himself accountable for this tragic element. He will not, and does not, exclude himself from blame. For love's sake God embraces the failed responsibility of human beings and "comes down" (Gen 11:5) into the violence of human activity to fully experience the pain of a partnership. He embraces us along with the brutality of our sin, to become sin and continues to suffer the consequence of it.

In the incarnation God, as Creator, chooses to be a Creature. In the atonement God, as Victor, chooses to be Victim. God, as Judge, chooses to be judged. God, as wrath, takes human wrath into himself.[35] Because he freely and graciously takes to himself the ultimate responsibility for the evil as well as the good we can say, in the words of King James Bible, "Though he slay me yet will I trust him" (Job 13:15).

> The cross is the place where suffering is allowed to exist, to be seen for what it is, completely and utterly meaningless and beyond what human explanation can contain. It is here, in the wider view offered from the cross, that love becomes possible, that it is possible to transcend patterns of abusing and being abused, to break the cycle of treating other human beings as objects of power.[36]

32. Polkinghorne, *Science and Christian Belief*, 81.
33. *CD* 3/3:289.
34. *CD* 3/3:310.
35. *CD* 4/1:185.
36. Watson, "A Wider View."

The Wrath of God Satisfied?

THE MYSTERY OF GOD

What more can we say about God? The awesome mystery of God can be safeguarded by a list of negatives. The God of Pastor Terry Jones is not God. The God maligned by Hitchens and Dawkins is not God. The metaphysical God of substance and theism is not God. The determinist divinity, who predestines everything and everyone, is not God. The God who sponsors child abuse is not God. The patriarchal male-God, who marginalizes women, is not God. The God who causes earthquakes in Haiti and elsewhere is not God. The God who flies into a rage when we upset him is not God. The God who fails to justify himself to us is not God.

Such false deities plague religion and theology. In the cross of Christ they are publicly declared to be fantasies, cheats, and liars.

Augustine was ever mindful of the mystery of God. There is a story told of how he was walking on the beach near Carthage puzzling over the Trinity. He had already written fifteen books on the *De Trinitate* and was no closer to fathoming the mystery. A little boy was running backwards and forwards across the sand with a pot. He filled the pot with sea-water and ran to pour it into a hole he had dug. He kept repeating the exercise. The bishop watched entranced. Finally he approached and asked, "What are you doing?" "I am trying to get that," said the lad, pointing to the sea, "into that," pointing to the hole in the sand. Augustine understood why he was unable to explain the mystery of the Trinity.

When reflecting of the mystery of God I have discovered that every question I ask raises more questions. I have also realized that not every question asked has an answer. One cannot capture the waves of the ocean in fishing net.

10

Wrath Satisfied

IN THE EARLY MONTHS of 2011, the democratic nations of the West watched in amazement as Arab dictators on the North African coast were driven out by ordinary people who, fed up with the oppression and corruption of the ruling elite, had taken to the streets. First to be liberated was Tunisia, and then Egypt. The chilling moment blighting this "Arab Spring" occurred when Colonel Muammar Gaddafi of Libya announced that he would not quit but would fight to the "last drop" of his blood. In table thumping rhetoric, he announced that his people loved him. He raved, "All you who love Muammar, go out on the streets. Secure the streets, chase them (the protestors), arrest them, hand them over to the security forces, they are terrorists . . . I will call on millions from one desert to another to purge Libya house to house . . . I'll still be running Libya when my Western foes have retired."

In the ensuing weeks he used pitiless mercenaries and salvoes of surface-to-surface missiles to obliterate towns and villages in wrathful vengeance upon his own people.

Gadaffi's wrath was being satisfied to safeguard his absolute power. Is this what we believe happens when we sing "the wrath of God is satisfied"? Cranfield, in his exposition of Romans 1:18 defines God's wrath as: "Indignation against injustice, cruelty and corruption, which is the essential element of goodness and love in a world in which moral evil is present."[1]

Paul's God has nothing in common with Gaddafi. God's wrath is not an outburst of uncontrollable rage arising from an obsession with power.

1. Cranfield, *Commentary on the Epistle to the Romans*, 109.

The Wrath of God Satisfied?

It is grace acting against sin in a legitimate way. It is an act, through which God satisfies the holy requirements of justice, to secure justice for all humanity. "Satisfaction" has to do with restoring a broken relationship.

THE DEMAND FOR SATISFACTION

We saw in chapter 4 how Tertullian (160–225) had to devise a disciplinary scheme to allow those Christians, who had fallen away during a time of persecution, to be again accepted within the church. We also noted in chapter 8 how the "Truth and Reconciliation Commission" used the principle of "satisfaction" to enable victims and oppressors to live together in the post-Apartheid South Africa.[2] The process was effective because deeply embedded, in Southern African cultures, is the holistic concept of "ubuntu" which creates an enormous capacity for forgiveness.[3]

The giving and receiving of "satisfaction" within a covenant relationship is part of a larger process of righting wrongs. Satisfaction involves acknowledging accountability, making restitution if necessary, and opening up ways for the healing of memories and full reconciliation. Satisfaction is about love being demonstrated corporately through justice being done, and publicly being seen to be done.

If we associate "giving satisfaction" with feudal knights in armor throwing down gauntlets because their honour has been impugned—as Anselm's theory might suggest—then we will be led astray. If we set it in a tight legal framework—as the theory of penal substitution does—then we will again misunderstand. Without some costly act of satisfaction in a fractured relationship, enmity becomes frozen. Even though God forgives all, human persons when deeply hurt find it hard to let go, forgive, accept forgiveness, and move on into a new future.

In our last chapter we saw that God embraces our failures, our fallen responsibility, our pain, and our shame. In addition God takes to himself/herself our failure to satisfy the holy requirements of justice. God, therefore, graciously satisfies justice within his own Trinitarian life. Christ satisfies God's righteousness, not because he died, and not because he was obedient unto death, but rather because he was "obedient unto

2. De Gruchy, *Reconciliation*, 183–184.
3. Stuckey, *Into the Far Country*, 27.

judgment."[4] Therein is the uniqueness of Jesus Christ. By such means is justice re-established and wholeness restored.

WHY DID JESUS HAVE TO DIE?

The Eastern and Western traditions of the church answer this question differently. The Eastern tradition, following Irenaeus, focuses on the incarnation. Christ leaves heaven and enters the prison house of this world to release us from Satan's captivity.[5] God (the *Logos*), by living out his life in a human body, initiates an unstoppable process of divinization. The resurrection is a declaration of victory over Satan and the powers of evil.

Why did Jesus have to die? It was not because God willed it, neither was it absolutely necessary for our salvation. Jesus died because wicked men sought to obliterate him and his mission. There is no need for an atoning sacrifice.[6] Compensation and satisfaction have no meaning.[7] All in all, the death of Christ is of secondary importance. This solution avoids all the difficulties posed by those theologians who argue that the Father, in sacrificing his Son, is guilty of unacceptable violence and of divine child abuse.

Although this explanation is very appealing it underplays the scandal of the cross and removes the divine "necessity" that Christ "must suffer" as the "servant of the Lord." While wishing to embrace features of this Eastern tradition, I do not think it goes far enough. In passing over the forensic elements it avoids the issue of justice. It fails to deal with the very root of the violence that disturbs our modern world.

The Western tradition assumes incarnation and resurrection as above, but focuses specifically on the death of Christ. This approach, advanced by Tertullian, Augustine, and Calvin,[8] uses all the ingredients of Isaiah 53. Augustine argued that when human beings sinned, God let them follow the path they had chosen. As God drew back Satan, who had already abandoned justice because of his obsession with power, rushed

---

4. Forsyth, *The Work of Christ*, 135.
5. Winter, *The Atonement*, 52.
6. Ibid., 25.
7. Ibid., 88.
8. *Inst.*II.xii.3.

The Wrath of God Satisfied?

in. God rescues us from the devil's power not by using more power but by re-establishing justice.

> Both devil and fallen men pursue power rather than righteousness (justice): but righteousness is the condition of power and not *vice versa* . . . Therefore the devil's power could only be overcome by righteousness.[9]

Christ, as the justice and righteousness of God, in being put to death releases humanity from a debtor's prison. The cross shows us that justice comes before power. Power is monistic, single, and retributive. Covenant justice is relational like the Trinity. Why did Jesus have to die? He died to demonstrate God's righteousness, restore justice to the planet, and heal its fragmented communities.

It was also necessary for Christ to die so as to proclaim the principle of sacrifice which was at work in the heart of God before the foundation of the world, and which continues to be enacted through space and time. Both traditions do this. They are not opposed to each other but complementary and contextual.

SIN, SATAN, AND WRATH.

For Abelard, and to some extent Julian, sin spoils a relationship between persons and leads us away from God. It is dysfunction and confusion. It obstructs, but does not ultimately negate the good.

René Girard (chapter 8), in explaining the dark trinity of violence, imitation, and scapegoating, tells us that Jesus did not die to appease God's wrath but rather to unmask and break humankind's repetitive cycle of violence. The only wrath is human wrath. He appears to agree with Julian who says,

> I saw no anger in God, neither for a short time nor for a long one; indeed, it seems to me that if God could be even slightly angry we could never have any life of place or being.[10]

If sin is viewed as dysfunction it follows that satisfaction is unnecessary and that God's wrath is a human projection.

---

9. Augustine, *Trinity*, XIII.4.
10. Julian, *Revelations of Divine Love*, LT.49, 112.

Paul, Anselm, Luther, and Calvin argue differently. Sin has objective reality. It can assume monstrous Gadaffi proportions. When threatened it fights back. It feeds the dark powers. It has to be forcibly removed (Matt 11:12). Sin is toxic because human beings keep replacing God with "empty gods" of their own. Satan uses these to intensify desire, distort reason, and tempt us with attractive opportunities to "self-destruct." A holy God has no alternative but to "hand us over" to become the playthings of the false gods and the delusions we have embraced (Rom 1:24–25). In one sense the dark powers are God's instruments of justice, in another they are his enemies, since they violate his rule and deface his image.

The Old Testament is clear that human suffering arises from human sinfulness and I have argued that God cannot be detached from this process. The destruction of Sodom and Gomorrah (Gen 19:24–25) is an extreme case of this. Even in this horrendous example of retributive justice, we must not be tempted to exclude God even though we may want to. God wills to be present even in his absence, since—as explained in the last chapter— "nothingness is the shadow side of his creating." If God, in Christ, is truly for us and with us, then the amount of pain and shame experienced by God in the destruction of Sodom and Gomorrah will be even more awesome than the event itself.

WRATH AND GOD'S COVENANT RELATIONSHIP WITH ISRAEL

We noted in chapter 1 that the Greek word *hilastērio*—translated "propitiation," "expiation," or "place of atonement"—was used to translate the Hebrew *kippēr* (Rom 3:25). *Hilastērion*, as propitiation, describes how something is done to appease God's anger.

When we dig deeply into the context of *kippēr* we unearth "covenant." A covenant is an arrangement in which two or more partners bind themselves to each other in a personal way for their mutual benefit. A covenant embraces partners. It is open ended and elastic enough to accommodate the shifts and failures of the partners. A contract, on the other hand, is essentially utilitarian, legally constructed, and based on hypothetical persons. It does not take account of the fluidity of human existence.

The Wrath of God Satisfied?

God makes a covenant with Israel. She was chosen to be the people of God not because of her strength but because of her weakness.[11] Her vocation is to be holy as God is holy and to mediate God's grace to the nations. This turns out to be a painful business since God holds Israel to this agreement by using the stick of wrath and the carrot of mercy. God's wrath, in the Old Testament, is directed against Israel far more than against the other nations, because without such coercion Israel would cease to be holy.

> The anger of the Lord was kindled against his people, and he stretched out his hand against them and struck them (Isa 5:25).

From Isaiah's perspective, God's wrath is enacted indirectly. God hands Israel over to the Assyrians. Assyria—like Gadaffi's elite Khamis brigade—is unable to restrain its own aggressiveness. Assyria, as the vehicle of God's wrath, will destroy itself through its own violence. All empires past, present, and future whether they are Babylon, Britain, the United States of America, or China will perish through their own self-aggrandizement in spite of the rhetoric they use. Even as Assyria triumphs, Babylon is waiting in the wings as the next instrument of wrath and will in turn suffer the same fate as Egypt. Wrath consumes wrath because justice rather than omnipotent power reigns supreme.

The Bible has another "take" on wrath. Zephaniah, in his prophetic poetry, allows no room for a human agency. God does it all from start to finish. "He will stretch out his hand against the north, and destroy Assyria; and he will make Nineveh a desolation" (Zeph 2:13). God's wrath is enacted directly.[12] In approaching the Old Testament in this way we must ever be aware that we are using the language of "evangelical imagination" rather than facticity.[13]

In these two perspectives, wrath is not a mechanistic or detached action. Wrath remains God's wrath. It has nothing to do with vindictive indignation or uncontrollable rage. Although such impressions can be found in the Old Testament's rhetoric of wrath, the firm and constant refrain is that God is "slow to anger" and his actions are bathed in "steadfast love" (Exod 34:6b). While the book of Hosea contains stinging rebukes

---

11. Stuckey, *Into the Far Country*, 50.
12. Brueggemann, *Out of Babylon*, 23–28.
13. Brueggemann, *David's Truth*, 14. Also *Interpretation and Obedience*, 23–24.

Wrath Satisfied

and warnings of impending judgment (Hos 11:1–7), God's heart recoils within him and tender compassion breaks through (Hos 11:8–9).[14]

All the ancient empires have passed away, undermined by their own self-aggrandizement and idolatrous power, yet Israel as a distinct people has survived for four thousand years. Her history is a story of suffering and endurance such that one writer, in contemplating the holocaust of the Second World War, says, "Israel seems to have been made a burnt-offering laden with the guilt of humanity".[15]

Because covenant is the basis of Israel's existence, vicarious suffering, wrath, propitiation and expiation illuminate her story. Her future servant role is described by the prophet Isaiah.

> We accounted him stricken, struck down by God and afflicted (53:4).
>
> The Lord has laid on him the iniquity of us all (53:6b).
>
> Yet it was the will of the Lord to crush him with pain (53:10a).
>
> He shall find satisfaction through his knowledge. The righteous one, my servant, shall make many righteous and shall bear their iniquities (53:11).

Present in these verses are all the difficult forensic elements of atonement, wrath (vss. 4, 10), substitution (vs. 6), satisfaction (vs. 11), and vicarious suffering.[16] If we set "satisfaction" within a legal or contractual framework, divine wrath become the instrument of retributive justice. If we place it within an understanding of covenant and "steadfast love," God's wrath becomes the instrument of restorative justice.

God's wrath directed against Israel should not be seen as punishment but rather as a disciplinary activity within the covenant to call her back to her primary vocation—mediating holiness. She has to learn, from the experience of the Exile, that the only way "of triumphal success and apparent progress . . . will be through suffering, and even rejection."[17]

> God works in Israel a way of reconciliation which does not depend on the worth of men or women, but makes their very sins in rebellion against him the means by which he binds them for ever to

---

14. Thompson, *God of Justice?*, 191.
15. Torrance, *The Mediation of Christ*, 38.
16. Groves, "Atonement in Isaiah 53," 88.
17. Thompson, *God of Justice?*, 187.

himself... in such a way that their true end is fully and perfectly realized.[18]

Jesus not only died for Israel, he is Israel. His baptism by John would be meaningless if this were not so. In attempting to understand propitiation, we must interpret sin, suffering, punishment, and wrath within a covenant perspective, always refusing to let contractual and legal factors influence the outcome.

PUNISHMENT AND PENAL SUBSTITUTION

Penal substitution follows when the forensic components are packed within a tight legal framework. Penal substitution is flawed for three reasons.

First, the advocates argue that it is Christ's punishment on the cross that sets us free from the curse of the law. This is not so. It is Christ's obedience unto judgment that releases us. Furthermore, Pilate's decision to pass the death sentence upon an innocent man is such a gross miscarriage of justice that it undermines the law.[19]

Second, nowhere in the New Testament is the crucified Christ said to suffer God's wrath, although such an interpretation can be imposed on some texts. Instead, Christ delivers believers from the "wrath to come" (1Thess 1:10; Rom 5:9). Within chronological history, wrath becomes active as God "hands people over" (Rom 1:24, 26, 28.) to partake of the "nothingness" they have chosen.

Third—and this goes to the heart—Hodge argues for penal substitution from the Adam and Christ analogy found in Romans 5:12—14, 18—19. Cranfield interprets this differently suggesting that any legal symmetry between Adam and Christ is blown apart by Paul's double affirmation of the "how much more" (*pollō mallon*) of Christ (Rom 5:15, 17).[20] Penal substitution is trapped in its own arithmetic. Its advocates are constrained, like the disciples of Jesus in Mark 8.17—21 who, when asked to reflect on the baskets of "left-overs" following the feeding of the 5000 and 4000, display a complete inability to comprehend the extravagance

---

18. Torrance, *The Mediation of Christ*, 29.
19. Weaver, "Response to Boersma," 85.
20. Cranfield, *Commentary on the Epistle to the Romans*, 269–290.

of grace.[21] I am contending that God continually lavishes such an abundance of goodness upon lost humanity that there is always a surplus. Penal substitution is a mechanical theory propounded by those, who, like the disciples scandalized by the women anointing the feet of Jesus with expensive ointment (Mark 14:3–7), think only in terms of numbers. They miss the fragrance of overflowing love.

In questioning penal substitution I am by no means dismissing the forensic elements. They are the necessary corollaries of love within a covenant relationship. As the writer of Hebrews puts it, "My child, do not regard lightly the discipline of the Lord, or lose heart when you are punished by him; for the Lord disciplines those whom he loves, and chastises every child whom he accepts" (Heb 12:5b–6).

"Love is not holy without judgment."[22] Restorative justice surpasses retributive justice because of the surpassing nature of God's love. Divine wrath safeguards a creative living space for humankind without which civilization would dissolve into barbarism and chaos. This we learnt from Anselm. The student who is constantly warned by his professor that he will fail the course if he does not do the required assignments cannot blame the professor if he fails. The wrath of God is intended to bring people to a border country in order to create a "liminal moment" not unlike God's action of taking Israel into the wilderness to purify her and prepare her as a new bride for the Lord (Hos 2:14–16).[23] God's wrath has nothing to do with retributive justice and everything to do with restorative justice. Because divine wrath is holy love in action it is not about punishment but about the renewal of truth and justice. Injustice excludes. Justice includes.

The Japanese theologian, Kazoh Kitamori describes the wrath of God as the reverse side of the pain and sorrow of God.[24] I too have argued that because the wrath is God's wrath, God suffers the pain of it. There is indeed a scorching flame of blame and shame within God.

In a final act of invasive surgery, God exposes us to his own hidden blistering fire of holy shame in the hope that this will to bring us to our senses and restore us. Like the Father of the prodigal son (Luke 15:11–23) God carries within himself the burden of allowing us to go our own way.

21. Brueggemann, *Mandate to Difference*, 157–158.
22. Forsyth, *The Work of Christ*, 85.
23. Countryman, *Living on the Border of the Holy*, 87.
24. Kitamori, *Theology of the Pain of God*.

The Wrath of God Satisfied?

Knowing that we can lose ourselves in the far country, God in Christ joins us there to seek and to save all who are lost. God's love extinguishes the fires of the wrath we generate. Divine wrath burns up the toxic materials of sin that threaten our violent destruction.

THE MESSAGE OF THE CROSS

On the cross God is revealed as the victor who chooses to be the victim, the judge who is judged, and the eternal pain-bearer. Christ's death proclaims the principle of sacrifice active in the heart of God before the foundation of the world, and now continually propagated through space and time. Alongside this, the resurrection of Christ changes the eschatological clock. The end-time triumph of God, where death is swallowed up in victory and wrath is absorbed in love, is also operating in the here and now of chronological time.[25]

The wrath of God destabilizes all triumphalism and destroys proud "theologies of glory," because God has refused to use power to defeat power and has chosen instead the holy path of self-emptying. The cross is scandalous because it questions the wisdom of the wise. It reveals humankind's obsession with power which adicts oppressive dictatorships, unaccountable hierarchical institutions and faceless bureaucracies. It tells us that these—like all Gadaffi figures—will ultimately destroy themselves through their own self-aggrandizement. Followers of Christ have no power only influence, no compulsion other than gentle persuasion. The cross is devoid of arrogance. It is a startling display of hope that, in the midst of dark corruption, frames our existence with new meaning.

I have argued that because God is Trinity, wrath cannot be detached from God but is the shadow side of his suffering love. God is not absolute power but relational righteousness. God's wrath is love in action against injustice, cruelty, and corruption in a violent world. God isn't wrathful in spite of being love; God is wrathful *because* God is love. Even the very highest and purest human wrath is at best a distorted and twisted reflection of the wrath of God.[26] Divine wrath unmasks human wrath. Wrath will consume wrath because, in God, justice rather than power has been satisfied. Divine wrath is a shadow cast by the light of hope.

25. Bartlett, *Cross Purposes*, 196-8.
26. Cranfield, *Commentary on the Epistle to the Romans*, 109.

11

Full Atonement Made

MICHAEL LAPSLEY IS AN Anglican priest in South Africa who, during the Apartheid years, came to see that if you were white and did nothing you were a functionary of the Apartheid Government. He joined the ANC. It was a warm sunny day in April. He was sitting at his desk with a pile of post in front of him, opening letter after letter. He tore off a cellophane cover and opened the magazine within—that was the mechanism that detonated the bomb. He lost an eye, his eardrums burst, and both his hands had to be amputated. At the Truth and Reconciliation Commission he said, "After the explosion I felt that it would have been better if I were dead, because now I am someone without hands . . . I have never before met a person without hands".

As he gives evidence he tries to wipe away his tears with his pincers.

> I do not see myself as a victim. I am living my life as meaningfully and joyfully as possible . . . I am not captured with hatred, because then they would have not only destroyed my body but my soul. Even without hands and an eye, I am much freer than the person who did this to me.[1]

On the cross Christ wins through because he "disregarded its shame" (Heb 12:2). Michael Lapsley's response to shame is similar. Although a victim, he has the victory.

In our last chapter we examined *hilastērion* as propitiation—something done within God to satisfy wrath and establish justice. In this

---

1. Krog, *Country of My Skull*.

chapter we explore *hilastērion as* "expiation"—something done for us to cover our sins, enable forgiveness, and transform our natures. Full atonement is divine therapy brought to completion in humankind.

GOD THE VICTIM, ABSORBING THE EVIL

In the chapter on Anselm, we saw how, through mutual sharing between Father and Son, God demonstrates himself to be both Victor and the Victim! God in Christ, out of his abundant love, freely chooses to be a victim.

In his remarkable book *The Stature of Waiting*, Vanstone reflects on Judas' action of betraying Jesus. This is the moment when our Lord's ministry ceases to be active and becomes passive (Mark 14:10). The word translated "betray"—*paradidomi*—literally means "to hand over." The same word is used of Pilate who hands Jesus over to be crucified (Mark 15:15).[2] Jesus is still the focus and centre of the story, but not the initiator of events. He receives and bears. "Jesus is no longer the one who does— He becomes the one who is done to."[3]

Jesus chooses to become a victim obedient unto death. He also makes himself a victim obedient unto judgment by choosing to subject himself to the distorted judgments of others, before submitting himself to the righteous judgment of God.

Mark's version of the crucifixion (Mark 15:21–39) demonstrates this process at work. The onlookers wag their heads and cry, "Aha! you who would destroy the temple . . . come down from the cross!" Present in this fickle crowd are the Romans and the chief priests. They are named because of their mutual antagonism. Normally they would be maligning each other—but not here. They are united in their desire to get rid of Jesus. Mark extends this malignant universalism by including all who pass by. The scapegoating mechanism is running at full blast, yet Jesus refuses to be against anyone. He is God for us. He absorbs all the "againstness" of persons who would normally be against each other. In this act, he both reveals and collapses the relentless machinery of violence.

But it is not simply Jesus who sucks out the evil. It is God. Jesus is not only in God, but God is in Christ, reconciling the world to himself. The

---

2. The same word is also used in Romans 1:24 where, in describing divine wrath, God "hands us over" to partake of the destruction we have chosen.

3. Vanstone, *The Stature of Waiting*, 22–23.

sum total of human violence is being absorbed into the life of the Trinity, where internal relationships are being stretched to breaking point, as God struggles to be victor over the contradiction while at the same time subjecting him/herself to it as victim.[4] The cross is the division of God from God to the utmost degree, while the resurrection is the union of God with God in the most intimate fellowship.[5] Wrath is being satisfied through love, which, because of its infinite nature, can never be satisfied until God has established his new creation. In this cosmic drama of wrath consuming wrath, suffering love redeems the powers of evil transforming "deadly violence into vital energy."[6]

Luther speaks of this as "a happy exchange" in which God in Christ, absorbs human sin into himself while, at the same time, bestowing upon us his gift of righteousness. Like Paul on the Damascus Road, although guilty we are no longer slaves of sin but have become slaves of Jesus Christ. Judgment has been pronounced. Condemnation belongs to the past. The dark powers of "nothingness" now lie behind us rather than before us. We are destined, in Christ, to fill our future days in sacrificial service and joyful acts of reparation as an outworking of restorative justice.

> In his crucifixion, Jesus absorbed the deprivation, the ambiguity, the suffering of the world, but when Jesus' absorption is viewed through the lens of resurrection, we are met with the gospel message that human beings and the structures we have built are incapable of having the last word.[7]

This happy exchange is not mechanical, legal, or metaphysical. It is covenantal and relational. He has become what we are so that we can become what he is.

THE DIVINE ADVOCATE

In 1 John 2:2, Jesus Christ is cast in the role of a divine advocate, pleading the cause of the sinner.

---

4. Barth, *CD* 4/1: 184–189.
5. Song, *Third-Eye Theology*, 61.
6. Moltmann, *The Trinity and the Kingdom of God*, 33.
7. Thompson, *Crossing the Divide*, 148.

> If anyone does sin. we have an advocate with the Father, Jesus Christ the righteous; and he is the (*hilasmos*)[8] atoning sacrifice (expiation) for our sins.

Jesus Christ is ably qualified for this task because he has enacted divine righteousness through his obedience unto judgment. This advocacy role is demonstrated in the Son interceding with the Father on our behalf.

J. McLeod Campbell, in his book *The Nature of the Atonement*, regards human beings as prodigal sons lost in a far country, alienated from their true home. Because Jesus has himself journeyed into the far country, he is able to intercede on behalf of all who are lost. Campbell thinks the prayer of John 17 to be a supreme illustration of this. On the cross Christ makes his soul an offering for sin. The offering consists of a perfect confession of sin, which is the "true and proper satisfaction to offended justice."[9]

> He (Jesus) responds to it (sin) with a perfect response—a response from the depths of that divine humanity—and in that perfect response He absorbs it. For that response has all the elements of a perfect repentance in humanity for all the sin of man—a perfect sorrow—a perfect contrition—and all the elements of such repentance, and that in absolute perfection.[10]

Although Campbell insists that it is God's gracious love that makes atonement he does not fully explain how Christ, who knew no sin, can make a perfect confession of sin.

Moberly states that one person can only be perfectly identified with another when that person is connected by nature and by love.[11] Because of love, it is the status of Christ as fully God and fully man, which qualifies him to be the "perfect" advocate. Athanasius knew this and struggled unceasingly for the *homoousion*, because he recognized that our very salvation was at stake if Jesus was not one with the Father.

Similarly, there can be no salvation unless God in Christ is truly human and identified in every way with fallen humanity, personally, individually, corporately, and vicariously. It was stated in our last chapter that Jesus is Israel and because of God's covenant relationship with Israel, their

---

8. *Hilasmos* is the person who accomplishes the expiation *hilastērion*.
9. Campbell, *The Nature of Atonement*, 122–126.
10. Ibid., 136.
11. Moberly, *Atonement and Personality*, 124–125.

history is summed up in Christ. Jesus is also everyman, everywoman, and every child because, in God's new covenant relationship, Jesus Christ draws all people to himself. Being without sin he attracts sin to become sin. Indeed God made him to be sin (2 Cor 5:21). Just as wrath should not be detached from God, so this vicarious principle of "sin bearing" should not be removed because if "love ceases to be vicarious, it will cease to be love."[12] Jesus Christ is not only one with humanity; he is one with the sin of humanity. Being one with the Father, the whole of the Godhead takes the blame, the shame, and the pain—suffering sin and absorbing it. Expiation is achieved because Jesus Christ, in fulfilling his role as the God-Man, becomes qualified to be the one and only advocate for humankind.

Bonhoeffer argues, in *Christology*, that the actions of the earthly Jesus do not prove his identity, they instead pose the question "who is this?" (Mark 4:41). Only through faith is insight given. "If I know who the person is who does this I know what he does."[13] The "who" of Jesus precedes the "what" and the "how" of salvation. This takes us back to Anselm, where faith comes before understanding.

Christ alone, because he is the judge judged in our place, and the victim condemned in our place, is also perfectly qualified to intercede for us. Moreover, through his resurrection and ascension, he becomes our advocate and intercessor for all time—past, present, and future.

THE GREAT INTERCESSOR

Christ is one with Abraham who pleads for the cities of Sodom and Gomorrah. He is Moses, who after the incident of the golden calf, prays that God would "blot him out" rather than destroy the people. He is the "servant" of Isaiah 53 who, "numbered with the transgressors", makes intercession for us. Jesus Christ is the mediator between God and humanity (1 Tim 2:5).

When did this intercessory ministry begin? While Campbell focuses on John 17, the letter to the Hebrews shows intercession permeating the whole life of Jesus (Heb 5:7). Intercession and petition, however, intensify within his passion until, on Golgotha, nearly all the words he utters are prayers inspired by the Old Testament Psalms.

12. Steward, *A Man in Christ*, 241.
13. Bonhoeffer, *Christology*, 40.

The Wrath of God Satisfied?

There is prayer for persecutors and those caught up in the killing machines of this world. There is intercession for those closest to him—his mother and the beloved disciple. His intercessions draw in the penitent thief—who represents all rioters, looters, and thugs. The final prayers from the cross take us into the heart of the Trinity exposing the tension of separation. "My God, my God, why have you forsaken me?" (Matt 27:46), provides a window into the relationship of Father and Son— a relationship strained to breaking point, as the being of God is flooded with wrath and sin. The arms of God are being stretched, in tortured pain, to embrace a violent world.[14] He who knew no sin has become sin. The estrangement and the god-forsakenness of all humanity is encapsulated in that terrible cry of dereliction. The totality of global pain is being absorbed.

It would be a mistake to think that God, the Father, listens passively to the anguished cry of his Son. Because each partner within the Trinity shares fully in the person of the other, the response of the Father will mirror that of the Son. As the Son yells his god-forsakenness at the Father, the Father —like the father of the lost son who looks towards the far country (Luke 15)—prays, "My Son, my beloved Son, where are you?" Pain, passion, and petitions fly across the void of "nothingness" robbing it of its existence. Prayer, within the Trinity, fills the void establishing full at-one-ment. This is declared in the great shout of the Father in the Son—"It is finished," and the Son to the Father —"Into thy hands I commend my Spirit." Thus the absence of God is filled with the presence of God, and the black hole of evil is transformed into a blazing quasar of creativity. The arms of God, once stretched to breaking point, come together to embrace all humanity. The resurrection is the sign of God's eternal hug.

Although this, undoubtedly, is the decisive moment in time, the universal application of the atoning event is set in motion when Christ is crowned as King, and "sits at the right hand" of the Father to fulfill his eternal priestly role.[15] In the old covenant, Moses climbs a mountain to intercede for Israel. In the new covenant, Christ makes intercession for us (Rom 8:34) from this exalted position. His entry into the eternal "holy of holies" serves notice on all earthly temples: they are now replaced by his resurrection body (Heb 7:2425). The eternal sacrifice before time has

---

14. The cry of dereliction hardly ever appears in feminist readings of the cross (Moltmann-Wendel, "Is there a Feminist Theology of the Cross?," 92) "Godforsakenness" is not easily compatible with a God who is regarded as entirely immanent within the world.

15. Cocksworth, "The cross, our worship and our living," 115–116.

now been ratified in time. The intercessory work of God, revealed in time by cross and resurrection, is now efficacious for all time. Expiation, as full atonement, has been accomplished.

This enables the Spirit, with groaning too deep for words, to bring into every global situation the abundant life, which has been made available for all, through the propitiatory acts of God in Christ.

> The death of the Son and the separation of God from God in the cry of dereliction on the cross, give way to a new birth, the *ekstasis* which is the mission of the Spirit.[16]

Only God can know God, and only God can reveal himself through himself. This is the work of the Holy Spirit who—as the new advocate (John 14:16, 26; 15:26)—implants the intercessory work of Christ for us, with us and in us.[17] "Calvary is the possibility of Pentecost and Pentecost is the realization in the human spirit of Calvary."[18] The mission of the church following Pentecost is to discern what the Spirit is doing in the world and, as a covenant partner with God, joining in.[19] When this happens an energy exchange takes place. Divine nature begins to be restored to humanity because, in Christ, our humanity is forever lodged in God.

MISSION, MARK, AND DISCIPLESHIP

All the writers considered in this book insist that, because of what God has done in Christ, evil is conquered and all shall be well. The news on our television screens, however, clearly negate this. Leonardo Boff says, "a glance at history reveals the stubborn presence of an anti-history—a history of evil, suffering, violence, and crime of immense dimensions."[20] What then has atonement achieved? It has launched a Pentecostal discipleship of hope.

> Wherever people seek the good, justice, humanitarian love . . . there we can say, with all certainty, that the resurrected one is

---

16. Soskice, *The Kindness of God*, 117.
17. Torrance, *The Mediation of Christ*, 115–119.
18. Moberley, *Atonement and Personality*, 152.
19. Stuckey, *On the Edge of Pentecost*, 6.
20. Boff, *Passion of Christ, Passion of the World*, 102.

present, because the cause for which he lived, suffered, was tried and executed is being carried forward.[21]

What the powers of evil did not anticipate was that an infinite flood of new life would be released into the world following Christ's death and resurrection. They did not foresee that the end-time of release and redemption would enter into the chronological time of the here and now.

Mark's Gospel does not end with a triumphal resurrection or a Pentecost. Instead it leaves us trembling on the edge of costly discipleship. Mark is showing us that the person and the work of Jesus can only be fully experienced through a discipleship, which necessitates a painful process of "stripping down." Mark shows us how Jesus peals off the comforting illusions of the disciples. Disciples, like blind Bartimaeus, have to cast aside their garments to follow in the way (10:50–52). Discipleship is portrayed as leaving cloaks and clothing behind (13:16). Even the young man in the garden has his nightshirt torn off (14:51) and the final shreds of Peter's ego are ripped away in the courtyard of denial leaving him naked and ashamed (14:72b).[22] The nearer we get to the cross and resurrection, the more our vulnerability is exposed.

Mark applies the same imagery to Jesus, who exchanges his active ministry for one of passive endurance. He is stripped of his royal robe of mockery. His own garment is gambled away and the last shreds of clothing torn from his body, making him a naked object of shame and degradation. His awareness of the Father is also ripped away as he, the object of sin and wrath, plumbs the depth of separation. Thus the flesh of his humanity finally exposes the humanity of God's divinity (Mark15:39). Finally the veil of the temple is torn down to reveal the emptiness of human religion. These climactic events change all the default settings of religion by recasting earthly petitions within the priestly interactions of the Trinity.

Prayer, in Mark's Gospel, is fully integrated into discipleship. "The brevity of Mark's stories and teaching about prayer should not deceive us into thinking that prayer is unimportant in the Gospel narrative."[23] Mark alone gives us the graphic picture of Jesus sighing and looking up to

---

21. Boff, *Jesus Christ Liberator*, 219.
22. Burdon, *Stumbling on God*, 88–90.
23. Hinks, *God's Passion*, 28.

heaven before uttering the words "Ephphatha"—"be open" (7:34). Mark wants everyone to look up, hear and speak.

THE ETERNAL SACRIFICE

Because discipleship is about stripping down—God-fulfillment through self-denial—it is essentially sacrificial. In following Christ's way of obedience, the illusions of the world are ripped away both to expose sin and reveal the potential of the Kingdom of God. Nowhere is this message made more explicit than in the sacraments of the church. "They identify us with the Redeemer's Sacrifice and, by virtue of that identification, enable us to have fellowship with his sufferings and to dedicate ourselves to God as living sacrifices."[24]

The cross shows us that ultimately evil destroys evil and that the sacrificial way will triumph. At the close of Michael Lapsley's testimony, Desmond Tutu said, "I give to God glory for you Michael, and I am thankful for you . . . because you can talk of the crucifixion and the resurrection, because it is in your body."

The eternal principle of sacrifice revealed though the self-limitation of God in Christ is exemplified in the lives of people like Michael Lapsley. In his own pursuit of justice he was stripped down to the core of his being as the bomb ripped away parts of his body. Suffering and martyrdom are not incidental to the mission of the church—they drive the mission.

Sacrifice is fertility and blood. John, in his Gospel, mentions the pierced side of Jesus from which water and blood flow. This is the image of giving birth in pain.[25] Blood is love in solution. Sacrifice must again become the animating principle of Christian discipleship if the defaced image of God is to be restored within humanity. Only then will full atonement be complete.

---

24. Whale, *Victor and Victim*, 139.
25. Watson, "A Wider View."

EPILOGUE

Atonement Today and Tomorrow

12

Outside a City Wall

It was one of those occasions in Britain, when the churches at the city center managed to put on a public display of unity. Even though the waving daffodils in the small park signaled the arrival of spring, there was a biting chill in the air.

We were a motley gathering of about fifty stalwarts including a few children, three pushchairs, one wheel chair and a dog. If all the members of the central churches had decided to come, we would have numbered nearly a thousand. Strange how a cold breeze, on an Easter weekend, and procession of witness can freeze Christian devotion![1]

There was however no lack of the devotion in the milling throng we encountered in the High Street as they stocked up for the Easter weekend. In the shopping mall our procession had to fight its way through a heaving hubbub of shoppers. How does one compete with the pungent smell of coffee and the warm enticing interiors of shops selling chocolate eggs and Easter fripperies? Our mournful march was a blot on the consumer landscape. Buying and selling was the name of the game. What we were

---

1. Acts of worship and witness in the open air have been a feature of church life in Britain even before John Wesley preached beyond the walls of the church. Following the 1914–1918 war, open air services of remembrance took place annually around war memorials scattered throughout the land. These occasions became increasingly ecumenical. As congregations dwindled, during the middle years of the twentieth century, various forays beyond the church building continued to be made by struggling congregations in a vain attempt to communicate with those who, still believing in God, no longer came to church. The procession of witness, described above, was one such feeble attempt. It took place in 2002 and was not repeated.

offering was not on the list of "must-haves." We stopped, huddled, and began to sing.

> There is a green hill far away,
> Outside a city wall,
> Where the dear Lord was crucified,
> Who died to save us all.[2]

The "green hill" was certainly far away and the bustling crowd seemed uninterested in salvation. The question of why Jesus had to die would not have entered their heads. We were out of place. We belonged far away outside the city wall.

Before we moved on, I glanced into a bookshop. My attention was drawn to a novel on display. I took a closer look. My eyes had not deceived me. The title of the book was "Atonement."[3] It seemed that the cross of Christ was not entirely missing from this cathedral of consumerism.

A SHOPPER'S PARADISE?

Andrew Marr, at the end of his six hundred page *History of Modern Britain*, concludes, "this history has told the story of the defeat of politics by shopping" aided by the "great car economy."[4] Descartes (1596–1650), one of the founding fathers of the "modern" period of history, coined the statement "I think therefore I am" (*cogito ergo sum*). A person's identity was to be defined through "thinking." Today, many people in the Western World establish their identity through what they buy. Has retail therapy therefore become the contemporary atonement theory?

Oliver James suggests that the modern shopper is suffering from a sickness called affluenza. It is a product of consumerism. Affluenza destroys our ability to discriminate between what we want and what we need, and increases our susceptibility to emotional disorders.[5] Retail therapy, it seems, does not deliver atonement.

The man who wrote the Old Testament book of Ecclesiastes reached the same conclusion. Tradition identifies him as King Solomon. Having had everything, and tried everything, he concludes that it is all empty and

2. *MHB*, 180.
3. McEwan, *Atonement*.
4. Marr, *History of Modern Britain*, 597.
5. Oliver, *Affluenza*.

meaningless. Nowhere else in the Bible is the word "I" used as many times as in this first chapters of Ecclesiastes.[6] The message is clear; meaning is not found in an "I" centered life.

A person's sense of guilt used to be the point of contact for the Gospel. The popular evangelists of my youth began their message with judgment and worked on our guilty fears to present Christ as the solution—as still happens in many places. During the 1950s in Britain, "doubt" rather than "guilt" became the point of contact. The thoughtful apologist began to replace the emotional evangelist. Within our violent contemporary culture, guilt and faith are out; anxiety and debt are in. Sin, however, remains as toxic as ever and is demonstrated by the "stingy, fearful, consumptive self that will stop at nothing in its self-absorption."[7] In societies where such anxious, self-absorbed individuals clamor for their right to "have it all" violence will inevitably occur.

PENAL SUBSTITUTION.

The ideas and metaphors within penal substitution readily connect with people living in a violent, anxious and debt-ridden society. John Stott—a British advocate of penal substitution—examines the metaphor of debt and argues that Christ died to pay "the wages of sin" which is death (Rom.6:23).[8] He concludes that human death is not a *natural* event but a *penal* event. Certainly in our violent world many deaths are not natural. They are the co-lateral of war and injustice. I have argued that the principle of sacrifice is embedded by God within his creation therefore, if we exclude untimely terminations, death is not a penal event but rather an essential ingredient of what it is to be human. Stott's interpretation of debt is not the whole story.

Christina Baxter, in her re-appraisal of penal substitution, looks at the issue of debt in a very different way.

> God has chosen to carry the penalty himself so that it becomes his passion. A very carefully refined penal idea of atonement has moved from the image of penalty as punishment to the image of penalty as costliness or debt.[9]

---

6. Sacks, *Celebrating Life*, 48.
7. Brown, *Cross Talk*, 118.
8. Stott, *The Cross of Christ*.
9. Baxter, "The Cursed Beloved," 72.

The Wrath of God Satisfied?

She says the idea of "being bought with a price" has a particular application for women's salvation. Such a metaphor of redemption "gives me a sense of worth and value" and draws the sting from the condemnation of others.[10] Her line of enquiry not only provides a different perspective on debt but, when set alongside Stott's interpretation, suggests that men and women experience the cross differently.

WOMEN, MEN, DEBT, AND BLOOD

Elizabeth Moltmann-Wendel examines this difference.

> The Abrahamic religions, with their approach from the need to depart from the father's house, have legitimized a secret contempt for origins . . . To become a man, it is necessary to leave one's origins, but that brings a feeling of guilt; it can be experienced as godlessness, since the goal is unattainable.[11]

A man achieves and discovers himself and God by seeking what is transcendent or beyond. A woman, by contrast, lives with God by being in tune with the person she already is. Moltmann-Wendel attempts to resolve the either/or tension as she reflects, from Mark's Gospel, upon the male disciples (14:50) and the women (16:8)—both of whom "flee." The disciples, in the garden, abandon their hero because he shames them by passively allowing himself to be arrested. The women, on the other hand, maintained solidarity with the passive Jesus but, filled with fear, run away when they hear of the resurrection. Moltmann-Wendel concludes that for women, unlike men, discipleship is not de-railed by the cross but by the resurrection. "Their immanence had holes made in it through the experiences of transcendence."[12] Men live out of transcendence; women out of immanence. These differences in perception are complementary. Cross and resurrection, strength and weakness, filling and emptying, the active and the passive are, in John's Gospel, part of the same lifting up (3:14, 12:32). Both are the necessary corollaries of the life of obedience.

Other features of atonement are affected by gender. "Blood" for men is linked with invasion and violence. "Blood" for women is the ever-present symbol of fertility and life. The endless stream of violent stories and

---

10. Baxter, "Jesus the Man and Women's Salvation," 144.
11. Moltmann-Wendel, "Feminist Theology of the Cross," 89.
12. Ibid., 97.

images which flash across our news screens should tell us that we cannot dispense with the metaphor of "blood." Moreover, in a hard-pressed economy, we cannot ignore the metaphors of "debt" and "sacrifice" which also play differently for men and women. One of the conclusions of this book is that sacrifice must again become an essential feature of Christian discipleship. Sadly we have become so used to cheap credit that our capacity either to wait or to sacrifice ourselves has been eroded. Rediscovering these virtues will be painful.

When we look at Augustine and Julian—both of whom lived in troubled times—we again find two different perspectives. The body with its desires and passions was a problem for Augustine. This was not so with Julian who was interested in the body.[13] Even though this affected their understandings of sin and wrath both, believing that the people of God were predestined before the foundation of the world, believed that ultimately all would be well. For Augustine, the glass is half empty. For Julian, the glass is half full.

THEORIES AND STORIES

Of the theorists considered in part one; it is Anselm who best addresses the challenges of today. He lived in a violent period of history and recognized how honorable institutions protect civilized life from the rampaging forces of lawlessness and chaos. He also addressed the issue of debt but explored it in the light of God's tender love and compassion. God's extravagant gift of grace in Christ satisfies all the demands of justice and swallows up wrath in mercy. Anselm does not advance a wooden theory but, through a process of dialogue, gives us an explanation of incarnation and atonement that is bathed in praise and prayer.

If, from Anselm's insights, we are to create a contemporary atonement theory, four factors should be kept in mind:

1. Because God is Trinity, metaphysical concepts are largely inappropriate. A contemporary theory needs to employ relational language.
2. The theory should proceed from a theological understanding of his "wrap-around Trinity" lest Father and Son be set over and

---

13. Soskice, *Kindness of God*, 139.

against each other.

3. The theory needs to be emptied of legal, punitive, and contractual content and be shaped by a Biblical understanding of God's covenants, old and new.
4. The message of the cross registers differently to different people. Gender issues are significant.

When an atonement theory is re-worked in this way it begins to resemble a story. This should not surprise us. All the theories considered in part one were based on Scriptural passages as the church, because of some internal problem or external challenge, tried to explain how the death and resurrection of Jesus could bring hope and healing to a troubled situation. It has been said that those, who created the theories, often by-passed the actual stories of the evangelists and thus distorted the primary narrative. This suggests that we should give more weight to the narrative tradition of Scripture.[14]

A creative connection between Scripture, theory, and story has been assumed in this book. That is why I begin each chapter with a story and provide cameo sketches of the theologians who advanced the theories. It is relatively easy in some cases to co-relate Scripture, a modern story, and a theory—as in chapter 2, with the Robben Island incident and the *Christus Victor* theory. It is much harder to find a story or preach a sermon to illustrate how the wrath of God is satisfied—though I shall attempt to do so in the concluding sermon.

In an age of "sound-bites" we can be tempted to opt for "easy" texts or "thin" narratives. It is here that the traditional "crown jewels" make a significant contribution since they, as a priceless resource, put us in touch with the sacrificial experience of creative Christians who wrestled with Scripture. The crown jewels are essential because they give "gravitas" to sermons about the cross. Furthermore, thin narratives and easy sermons will do little for congregations unless "the other" becomes a dynamic ingredient. "Self stories" will not release us.[15] The real self only emerges through a liminal experience of crucifixion and resurrection, which confronts and transcends the self. The traditional atonement presentations are certainly not lacking in their references to "the other." If the church is

---

14. Wright, *Jesus and the Victory of God*, 541–543.
15. Mann, *Atonement for a 'Sinless' Society*, 86–98.

to rediscover the rich potency of the crown jewels, we have to de-center our own perspectives of self-interest. This necessitates a sacrificial stripping-down process.

Post-modernists tend to pour scorn on meta-narratives even though it has been argued that they have their own meta-narrative.[16] Brueggemann reminds us that the Bible, although assumed by some to contain one meta-narrative, is rather made up of many narratives that do not always harmonize.[17]

Presentations of atonement in our contemporary culture can be discovered beyond the walls of the church. On our procession of witness I was delighted to see Ian McEwan's *Atonement* in the shopping emporium. Novels like Khaled Hosseini's *The Kite Runner* or Christina Lamb's *House of Stone* contain atonement images and ideas, as do popular films like *The Shawshank Redemption* and *Amistad*. Theological reflections on atonement, some better than others, can still find their way into the shopping mall and the cinema. Popular novels and films of this sort become even more effective if the narrator, author, or producer has been influenced by "the crown jewels" of the church. Ralph Wood in his *The Gospel According to Tolkien* shows how *The Lord of the Rings* is really an imaginative reworking of atonement theology in the context of "a culture of death." "Rather than grinding our faces in these horrors . . . (Tolkien's book) suggests a cure for the ills of our age. This great work enables us to escape *into* reality."[18]

THEOLOGY, ANSELM, AND SERMON

In my last book *On the Edge of Pentecost*, I argued that God is seeking to transform the church in Britain into the vibrant vehicle of God's tomorrow rather than preserving it as the museum piece of his yesterday.[19] Radical change is required if the traditional churches are not to be wiped off the landscape. Given the advance of secularism and militant atheism in Britain, the survival of Christianity depends on every church member becoming a disciple (learner) and every disciple a theologian. Being a

16. Alsford, "Atonement and the Post-Modern Deconstruction of the Self," 203–205.
17. Brueggermann, *The Bible and Postmodern Imagination*, 70.
18. Wood, *The Gospel according to Tolkien*, 1.
19. Stuckey, *On the Edge of Pentecost*, 6.

theologian means three things. First you have a story to tell. Second you are constantly open and obedient to the Holy Spirit. Third, you are able to download the immeasurable riches of God's grace. This book focuses on the latter. Strictly speaking, God's grace downloads itself because of the cross and resurrection of Jesus Christ.

In this the preacher has a key role to play. The sermon brings together biblical narrative, Word, and Spirit to initiate a dialogue between God, the preacher and the congregation. Stephen Holmes believes that Anselm can teach us much about preaching the atonement.[20] "Our congregations are not worried about the involvement of the eternal God in time, but the involvement of the loving God in violence, does concern them."[21]

He believes that preachers have lost the ability to imagine new metaphors and concludes that Anselm is important because he did find a way of narrating "what Christ did on the cross that was so convincing that, essentially, it held sway until the Reformation."[22] It is the theologian's task to equip the preacher so that the preacher is able to confront the ills of society and inspire those who worship to become committed disciples, prepared to go all the way with Christ and "make the sacrifice complete."

---

20. Holmes, "Cur Deus Po-mo?"
21. Ibid., 9.
22. Ibid., 16.

THE SERMON

Trees of Tragedy and Triumph

"He went and hanged himself." (Matt 27:5)

THIS IS NOT A very promising text. I can hardly conclude this sermon with the words of Jesus, "Go and do likewise." The recent tragic deaths of Amy Winehouse and Whitney Houston, however, suggest that it is possible to become so severely damaged by fame, fortune and the expectations of others that untimely death follows almost as a natural consequence.[1]

Within a consumer celebrity culture, many put themselves under intense pressure to succeed, make money, and to climb to the top of the tree. Jack Higgins, a very successful thriller writer, was once asked what it is like when you finally make it. He said, "When you get to the top, there is nothing there."

Judas, the disciple, is an enduring enigma. As far as we can ascertain he was high up in our Lord's affections. He was probably lying next to Jesus at the last supper. How else could Jesus have acknowledged him as the betrayer without the other disciples hearing (Matt.26:25)? It has been suggested that Jesus not only gave him the choicest morsel of food but may even have placed it in his mouth (John 13:30). It was love's last appeal, but tragically Judas had drunk so much darkness into his soul that this token of love was received as wrath. None of the other disciples suspected his dark designs as he left the upper room on the night of betrayal. He was a trusted companion, sent on a special mission by Jesus (John 13:29–30). Alan Mann thinks that many today unconsciously take Judas as their role model. "He typifies the post-industrial self . . . the intimacy Judas craves is purely for his own satisfaction and that others are expendable."[2]

Matthew, in his Gospel, invites us to consider the two ways of discipleship. There is the narrow road leading to life, and there is the broad road—which Judas takes—leading to destruction (Matt 7:13). We have

---

1. Amy Winehouse was found dead on 23 July 2011, and Whitney Houston on 11 February 2012.

2. Mann, *Atonement for a 'Sinless' Society*, 125.

The Wrath of God Satisfied?

the same choice. We can like the priests, in the final chapter of Matthew, hide from reality and live a lie (28:11–15); or we can worship Jesus and go as obedient disciples to live in his Kingdom presence.

Both Jesus and Judas die "hanging on a tree" (Acts 5:30, 10:39, 13:29). In the eyes of the law both are cursed. The contrast between Jesus and Judas could not have been greater. The life and death of Judas demonstrates the "down-side" of God's justice, enacted in wrath. The death of Jesus demonstrates the "up-side" of God's justice, enacted in love.

Judas is the antithesis of Jesus.[3] While the Jesus narrative is one of coherence, his is a narrative of incoherence. Judas slips into the "nothingness" of isolation because he cannot maintain relationships. Jesus takes "nothingness" away from people, absorbing it into his own relational identity with the Father. Judas dies because he has based his whole life on an illusion and, losing all sense of self worth, suffers from chronic shame. He cannot confess, because confession would sink him further into shame. He cannot pray, because self-absorption has robbed him of the capacity to know anyone other than himself. He has distanced himself from the corporate world of relationships to such an extent that, when Jesus offers him a token of love, he turns away. The life and death of Judas is a negation of at-one-onement. He kills himself because he knows he is already dead. His suicide is the ultimate act of self-harming in a desperate attempt to feel something. Jesus and Judas represent two polarities; one walks the path to heaven, the other the path to hell! We have the same choice.

In Dante Alighieri's epic poem *The Divine Comedy* there is this inscription over the doorway of hell. "Justice it was that moved my great creator. Divine omnipotence created me and highest wisdom joined with primal love."[4]

Dante is suggesting that divine justice, power, wisdom, and love have created hell. Jesus and Judas illustrate the inseparable relationship between light and its shadow. Some argue that Dante's inscription points to the choices people make since love gives us the independence to freely decide on either path. I believe God is more directly involved. God, because of his love for the world, makes himself accountable for the "nothingness"—which is the hell of his "non-creating." Judas chose the path of

---

3. I am greatly indebted to Alan Mann's reflections on these respective narratives of coherence and incoherence. (Mann, 107–131).

4. Wilson, *Dante in Love*, 209.

"He went and hanged himself." (Matt 27:5)

"non-creating." In his quest for absolute power he copied the fall of the angels and dies on a tree. Jesus chose the path of creating. In his quest for justice he is obedient unto death and dies on a tree.

Jesus does not climb the tree like Judas; he is lifted up. In the Gospel of John, Jesus is not only lifted up on the cross, but he is raised up in resurrection. His cross becomes the new tree of life—not a tree of death.

Ours is still a world where people do irreparable damage to themselves, and to others, in their struggle to climb to the top. Ours is a world where people—like Judas—embrace the darkness of nothingness and self-destruct. In our world of suicides, violence, tragedy, and despair, it is not easy retaining a sense of hope.

There was a remarkable woman who lived many years ago in Norwich at a time when violence and death stalked the streets. For fifteen years she struggled to understand a vision she had seen of the crucified Christ. At last she received an answer. It is the secret of life.

> Do you want to know what your Lord meant? Know well that love was what he meant. Who showed you this? Love. What did he show? Love. Why did he show it to you? For love. Hold fast to this and you will know and understand more of the same.[5]

---

5. Julian, *Revelations of Divine Love*, LT.86, 179.

Bibliography

Abelard, Peter. "Exposition of Romans 3:19." In vol. 10, *The Library of Christian Classics*. London: SCM Press, 1956.
———. *The Letters of Abelard and Heloise*. Translated by Betty Radice. New York: Penguin, 1974.
Alsford, Michael. "Atonement and the Post-Modern Deconstruction of the Self." In *Atonement Today*, edited by John Goldingay, 203–221. London: SPCK, 1995.
Amos, Clare. *Beginning Over Again: Through Lent with Genesis and the Gospels*. Peterborough, UK: Inspire, 2005.
Anselm. *Cur Deus Homo (CDH)*. In *St. Anselm: Basic Writing*. Translated by S. N. Deane. La Salle, IL: Open Court, 1988.
———. "A prayer to St Mary to Obtain Love for Her and for Christ." In vol. 10, *The Library of Christian Classics*. London: SCM Press 1956.
Anatolios, Khaled. *Athanasius: The Coherence of his Thought*. London: Routledge, 1988.
Atkinson, James. *Martin Luther and the Birth of Protestantism*. London: Marshall Morgan and Scott, 1968.
Athanasius, "De Incarnatione Verbe Dei." In *St Athanasius on the Incarnation*. London: Mowbray, 1953.
Aulen, Gustaf. *Christus Victor*. Translated by S. G. Herbert. London: SPCK 1965.
Augustine. "The Trinity." In vol. 8, *The Library of Christian Classics*. London: SCM Press 1955.
Bainton, Roland. *Here I Stand: A Life of Martin Luther*. New York: Mentor, 1950.
Baker, Mark D., ed. *Proclaiming the Scandal of the Cross: Contemporary Images of the Atonement*. Grand Rapids: Baker Academic, 2006.
Barnes, Tom. *Atonement Matters: A Call to Declare the Biblical View of the Atonement*. Darlington, UK: Evangelical Press, 2008.
Barrow, Simon and J. Bartley, eds. *Consuming Passion: Why the Killing of Jesus Really Matters*. London: Darton, Longman and Todd, 2005.
Barrow, Simon. "The Cross, Salvation and the Politics of Satire." In *Consuming Passion: Why the Killing of Jesus Really Matters*, edited by S. Barrow and J. Bartley, 99–111. London: Darton, Longman and Todd, 2005.
Barth, Karl. *Church Dogmatics*, edited by G. W. Bromiley and T. F. Torrance. 14 vols. Edinburgh: T & T Clark, 1957-75.
Bartlett, Anthony. *Cross Purposes: The Violent Grammar of Christian Atonement*. Valley Forge, PA: Trinity Press International, 2001.
Bauckham, Richard. *Moltmann: Messianic Theology in the Making*. London: Marshall Morgan and Scott, 1987.

Bibliography

Baxter, Christina. "Jesus the Man and Women's Salvation." In *Atonement Today*, edited by John Goldingay, 131–147. London: SPCK, 1995.

———. "The Cursed Beloved: A Reconsideration of Penal Substitution." In *Atonement Today*, edited by John Goldingay, 54–72. London: SPCK, 1995.

Bell, Martin. *Through Gates of Fire: A Journey into World Disorder*. London: Weidenfeld and Nicolson, 2003.

Blocher, Henri. "The Atonement in John Calvin's Theology." In *The Glory of the Atonement: Biblical, Theological & Practical Perspectives*. Edited by Charles E. Hill and Frank A. James III, 279–303. Downers Grove, IL: InterVarsity, 2004.

Boersma, Hans. *Violence, Hospitality, and the Cross: Reappropriating the Atonement Tradition*. Grand Rapids: Baker Academic, 2004.

———. "Violence, The Cross, and Divine Intentionality. A Modified Reformed View." In *Atonement and Violence: A Theological Conversation*, edited by John Sanders, 47–69. Nashville: Abingdon, 2006.

Boff, Leonardo. *Jesus Christ Liberator: A Critical Christology for Our Time*. Maryknoll, NY: Orbis, 1978.

———. *Passion of Christ, Passion of the World: The Facts, Their Interpretation, and Their Meaning Yesterday and Today*. Maryknoll, NY: Orbis, 1987.

Bonhoeffer, Dietrich. *Christology*. London: Collins 1966.

———. *Letter and Papers from Prison*, London: SCM Press, 1954.

Bourke, Joanna. Review of *The Better Angels of Our Nature: Violence in History and its Causes* by Steven Pinker. In *The Times* (London) 10 October 2011.

Bouwsma, William. *John Calvin: A Sixteenth-Century Portrait*. New York: Oxford University Press, 1988.

Bradley, Ian. *The Power of Sacrifice*. London: Darton, Longman and Todd, 1995.

Brown, Robert McAfee. *Liberation Theology: An Introductory Guide*. Louisville: Westminster/John Knox, 1993.

Brown, Sally. *Cross Talk: Preaching Redemption Here and Now*. London: Westminster John Knox, 2008.

Brueggemann, Walter. *The Bible and Postmodern Imagination*. London: SCM Press, 1993.

———. *David's Truth: In Israel's Imagination and Memory*. Minneapolis: Fortress, 1985.

———. *Interpretation and Obedience: From Faithful Reading to Faithful Living*. Minneapolis: Fortress, 1991.

———. *Mandate to Difference: In Invitation to the Contemporary Church*. London: Westminster John Knox, 2007.

———. *Out of Babylon*. Nashville: Abingdon Press, 2010.

Brümmer, Vincent. *Atonement, Christology and the Trinity: Making Sense Of Christian Doctrine*. Aldershot, UK: Ashgate, 2005.

Brunner, Emil. *The Mediator: A Study of the Central Doctrine of the Christian Faith*. London: Lutterworth, 1959.

Burdon, Christopher. *Stumbling on God: Faith and Vision in Mark's Gospel*. London: SPCK, 1990.

Cable, Vince. *The Storm: The World Economic Crisis & What it Means*. London: Atlantic Books, 2009.

Calvin, John. *Institutes of the Christian Religion*. In vol. 20, *The Library of Christian Classics*. London: SCM Press 1961.

Campbell, John McLeod. *The Nature of the Atonement*, Cambridge: Clark, 1886.

Bibliography

Caputo, John. and Michael Scanion, eds. *God, the Gift, and Postmodernism*. Indiana Series in the Philosophy of Religion. Bloomington: Indiana University Press, 1999.

Chadwick, Owen. *A History of Christianity*. London: Orion, 1997.

Chalk, Steve and Alan Mann. *The Lost Message of Jesus*. Grand Rapids: Zondervan, 2004.

Civilisation: A Personal View by Kenneth Clark. Produced by John Murray. 13 episodes. London: BBC, 1969.

Cocksworth, Christopher. "The Cross, our Worship and our Living." In *Atonement Today*, edited by John Goldingay, 111–127. London: SPCK, 1995.

Cottret, Bernard. *Calvin: A Biography*. Edinburgh: T & T Clark, 2000.

Countryman, William. *Living on the Border of the Holy: Renewing the Priesthood of All*. Harrisburg, VA: Morehouse, 1999.

Cranfield, Charles E. B. *A Critical and Exegetical Commentary on the Epistle to the Romans: Introduction and Commentary on Romans 1–8*, vol. 1. The International Critical Commentary Series. Edinburgh: T & T Clark, 1975.

Daniels, Scott. "Passing the Peace: Worship that Shapes Nonsubstitutionary Convictions," In *Atonement and Violence: A Theological Conversation*, edited by John Sanders, 125–159. Nashville: Abingdon, 2006.

De Bourchgrave, Helen. *A Journey into Christian Art*. Oxford: Lion, 1999.

De Gruchy, John W. *Reconciliation: Restoring Justice*. London: SCM Press, 2002.

Dawkins, Richard. *The God Delusion*. London: Bantam, 2006.

Dillistone, F. W. *The Christian Understanding of the Atonement*. Welwyn, UK: Nisbet, 1967.

Dodd, C. H. *Letter to the Romans*. Moffet New Testament Commentary. London: Hodder and Stoughton, 1949.

Evans, G. R. *Anselm*. Outstanding Christian Thinkers. London: Chapman, 1989.

Fiddes, Paul. *Past Event and Present Salvation: The Christian Idea of Atonement*. London: Darton, Longman and Todd, 1989.

Farley, Wendy. *Tragic Vision and Divine Compassion: A Contemporary Theodicy*. Westminster John Knox, 1990.

Forsyth, Peter Taylor. *Positive Preaching and the Modern Mind*. London: Independent Press, 1964.

———. *The Justification of God: Lectures for War-Time on a Christian Theodicy*. London: Hodder & Stoughton, 1906.

———. *The Work of Christ*. London: Hodder & Stoughton, 1910.

Fox, Matthew. *Original Blessing*. New Mexico: Bear, 1983.

Fraser, Giles. "The Easter of Hawks, Doves, Victims and Victimisers." In *Consuming Passion: Why the killing of Jesus really matters*, edited by S.Barrow and J.Bartley, 12–18. London: Darton, Longman and Todd, 2005.

Ganoczy, Alexandre. *The Young Calvin*. Edinburgh: T & T Clark, 1987.

Gascoigne, Bamber. *The Christians*. New York: Morrow, 1977.

Girard, René. *I see Satan Fall like Lightening*. Translated by James G. Williams. Leominister, UK: Gracewing, 2001.

Goldingay, John. "Old Testament Sacrifice and the Death of Christ." In *Atonement Today*, edited by John Goldingay, 3–20. London: SPCK, 1995.

———. *Psalms 90–150*. Vol. 3 of *Psalms*. Baker Commentary on the Old Testament Wisdom and Psalms. Grand Rapids: Baker Academic, 2008.

Green, Joel B. and Mark D. Baker. *Recovering the Scandal of the Cross: Atonement in New Testament & Contemporary Contexts*. Illinois: IVP Academic, 2000.

Bibliography

Grey, Mary. *The Outrageous Pursuit of Hope: Prophetic Dreams of the Twenty-First Century.* London: Darton, Longman and Todd, 2000.

———. *To Rwanda and Back: Liberation Spirituality and Reconciliation.* London: Darton, Longman and Todd, 2007.

Groves, Alan. "Atonement in Isaiah 53." In *The Glory of the Atonement: Biblical, Theological & Practical Perspectives,* edited by Charles E. Hill and Frank A. James III, 61–89. Downers Grove, IL: InterVarsity Press, 2004.

Gruenler, Royce. "Atonement in the Synoptic Gospels and Acts." In *The Glory of the Atonement: Biblical, Theological & Practical Perspectives,* edited by Charles E. Hill and Frank A. James III, 90–105. Downers Grove, IL: InterVarsity Press, 2004.

Hengel, Martin. *Crucifixion.* London: SCM, 1977.

Hill, Charles E. and Frank A. James III, eds. *The Glory of the Atonement: Biblical, Theological & Practical Perspectives.* Downers Grove, IL: InterVarsity Press, 2004.

Hinks, Terry. *God's Passion: Praying with Mark.* Praying with the Gospels. Darton, Longman and Todd, 2011.

Hitchens, Christopher. *God is Not Great: How Religion Poisons Everything.* New York: Twelve, 2007.

Holmes, Stephen. "Cur Deus Po-mo? What St Anselm can Teach us About Preaching the Atonement Today." *Epworth Review* 36:1 (2009) 6–17.

Hosseini, Khaled. *The Kite Runner.* Bloomsbury, 2003.

Humphrys, John. *In God We Doubt: Confessions of a Failed Atheist.* Hodder & Stoughton, 2008.

Ibrahim, I.A. *A Brief Illustrated Guide to Understanding Islam.* Houston, TX: Dar-us-Salam, 1997.

Irenaeus. *Against Heresies.* In *Irenaeus of Lyons,* translated by Robert Grant. London: Routledge, 1997.

Jeffery, Steve, et al. *Pierced for Our Transgressions: Rediscovering the Glory of Penal Substitution.* Downers Grove, IL: InterVarsity, 2007.

Julian of Norwich. *Revelations of Divine Love.* Translated by Elizabeth Spearing. New York: Penguin, 1998.

Kelly, J. N. D. *Early Christian Doctrines.* London: Black, 1965.

Kennedy, Studdert. "The Sorrow of God." In *The Unutterable Beauty,* 129–135. London: Hodder & Stoughton, 1957.

King, Martin Luther. *Strength to Love.* London: Fontana, 1976.

Kitamori, Kazoh. *Theology of the Pain of God: The First Original Theology from Japan.* London: SCM, 1966.

Krog, Antjie. *Country of My Skull: Guilt, Sorrow, and the Limits of Forgiveness in New South Africa.* New York: Times Books, 2000.

Lamb, Christina. *House of Stone: The True Story of a Family Divided in War-Torn Zimbabwe.* London: Harper Perennial, 2006.

Lincoln, Andrew T. *Ephesians.* Vol. 42, Word Biblical Commentary. Nashville: Nelson, 1990.

Lohse, Bernard. *Martin Luther's Theology: Its Historical and Systematic Development.* Edinburgh: Augsburg Fortress, 1999.

Lovelock, James. *The Revenge of Gaia: Earth's Climate in Crisis and the Fate of Humanity.* New York: Lane, 2006.

Luther, Martin. *A Commentary on St Paul's Epistle to Galatians.* Translated by Philip S Watson. Westwood, NJ: Revell, 1972.

Bibliography

———. *Luther: Letters of Spiritual Counsel*. In vol. 28, *The Library of Christian Classics*. London: SCM Press 1955.

Mann, Alan. *Atonement for a 'Sinless' Society: Engaging with an Emerging Culture*. Faith in an Emerging Culture. Exeter, UK: Paternoster, 2005.

Marr, Andrew. *History of Modern Britain*. London: Macmillan, 2007.

Marshall, I. Howard. *The Gospel of Luke*. The New International Greek Testament Commentary Series. Exeter, UK: Paternoster, 1978.

Mathewes-Green, Frederica. "Rising Victorious." In *Proclaiming the Scandal of the Cross: Contemporary Images of the Atonement*, edited by Mark D. Baker, 42–45. Grand Rapids: Baker Academic, 2006.

McCulloch, Diarmaid. *Christian History: An Introduction to the Western Tradition*. Peterborough, UK: Epworth, 2006.

McEwan, Ian. *Atonement*. New York: Vintage, 2002.

McFague, Sallie. *The Body of God: An Ecological Theology*. Minneapolis, MN: Fortress, 1993.

McGrath, Alister. *Christian Theology: An Introduction*. Oxford: Blackwell, 2000.

———. *A Life of John Calvin*, Oxford: Blackwell, 1990.

McGrath, Alister, and Joanna McGrath. *The Dawkins Delusion: Atheist Fundamentalism and the Denial of the Divine*. London: SPCK, 2007.

McIntyre, John. *The Shape of Soteriology: Studies in the Doctrine of the Death of Christ*. Edinburgh: T & T Clark, 1992.

Moberly, Robert C. *Atonement and Personality*. London: Murray, 1901.

Morris, Colin. *Snapshots: Episodes in a Life*. Peterborough, UK: Inspire, 2007.

Moses, John. *The Sacrifice of God: A Holistic Theology of Atonement*. Norwich: Canterbury Press, 1992.

Moltmann, Jürgen. *The Crucified God*. London: SCM, 1974.

———. *The Trinity and the Kingdom of God*. SCM, 1983.

Moltmann-Wendel, Elizabeth. "Is there a Feminist Theology of the Cross?" In *The Scandal of a Crucified World*, edited by Yacob Tesfai, 87–98. Maryknoll, NY: Orbis, 1994.

Murray, Stuart. "Rethinking Atonement after Christendom." In *Consuming Passion: Why the Killing of Jesus Really Matters*, edited by Simon Barrow & Jonathan Bartley, 27–35. London: Darton, Longman and Todd, 2005.

Northcott, Michael. "Atonement, Violence and Modern Imperial Order." In *Consuming Passion: Why the Killing of Jesus Really Matters*, edited by Simon Barrow & Jonathan Bartley, 89–98. London: Darton, Longman and Todd, 2005.

O'Leary, Daniel. "Caught between Earth and Heaven." *The Tablet*, April 15, 2006.

Oliver, James. *Affluenza*. London: Vermilion, 2006.

Paffenroth, Kim. *Judas: Images of the Lost Disciple*. Louisville, KY: Westminster John Knox, 2001.

Primavessi, Anne. *From Apocalypse to Genesis: Ecology, Feminism, and Christianity*. Kent, UK: Burns and Oates, 1991.

Polkinghorne, John. *Science and Christian Belief: Theological Reflections of a Bottom-Up Thinker*. London: SPCK, 1994.

Ray, Darby K, *Deceiving the Devil: Atonement, Abuse, and Ransom*. Cleveland, OH: Pilgrim, 1998.

Reed, Charles. *Just War?: Changing Society and the Churches*. London: SPCK, 2004.

Bibliography

Richards, Anne. "Being Delivered from Gibson's Hell." In *Consuming Passion: Why the Killing of Jesus Really Matters*, edited by Simon Barrow & Jonathan Bartley, 74–80. London: Darton, Longman and Todd, 2005.

Richardson, Neil. *Paul for Today: New Perspectives on a Controversial Apostle*. London: Epworth, 2009.

Roth, John. "A Theodicy of Protest." In *Encountering Evil: Live Options in Theodicy*, edited by Stephen Davis. Edinburgh: T & T Clark, 1981.

Rupp, Gordon. *The Righteousness of God: Luther Studies*. The Birkbeck Lectures in Ecclesiastical History. London: Hodder & Stoughton, 1953.

Sacks, Jonathan. *Celebrating Life: Finding Happiness in Unexpected Places*. London: Continuum, 2004.

Sanders, John, ed. *Atonement and Violence: A Theological Conversation*. Nashville: Abingdon, 2006.

Schmiechen, Peter. *Saving Power: Theories of Atonement and Forms of the Church*. Grand Rapids: Eerdmans, 2005.

Selby, Peter. *Grace and Mortgage: The Language of Faith and the Debt of the World*. London: Darton, Longman and Todd, 1997.

Song, Choan-Seng. *Third-Eye Theology: Theology in Formation in Asian Settings*. London: Lutterworth, 1980.

Spong, John Shelby. *Why Christianity Must Change or Die: A Bishop Speaks to Believers In Exile*. San Francisco: Harper, 1998.

Soskice, Janet Martin. *The Kindness of God: Metaphor, Gender, and Religious Language*. Oxford: Oxford University Press, 2007.

Southern, Richard. *St Anselm: A Portrait in a Landscape*. Cambridge: Cambridge University Press, 1990.

Stauffer, Ethelbert. *New Testament Theology*. Translated be John Marsh. London: SCM, 1963.

Steward, James S. *A Man in Christ: The Vital Elements of St. Paul's Religion*. London: Hodder & Stoughton, 1935.

Stott, John. *The Cross of Christ*. Downers Grove, IL: InterVarsity, 1986.

Stuckey, Tom. *Into the Far Country: A Theology of Mission for an Age of Violence*. Peterborough, UK: Epworth, 2003.

———. *On the Edge of Pentecost: A Theological Journey of Transformation*. Peterborough, UK: Inspire, 2007.

———. "The Crown Jewels of Faith." *Epworth Review* 36:1 (2009) 47–57.

———. "The Wrath of God Satisfied?" *Ichthus* 161:3, 4–7.

Sykes, Stephen. *The Story of Atonement*. Trinity and Truth. London: Darton, Longman and Todd, 1997.

Tesfai, Yacob, ed. *The Scandal of a Crucified World: Perspectives on the Cross and Suffering*. Maryknoll, NY: Orbis, 1994.

Thompson, Deanna. *Crossing the Divide: Luther, Feminism, and the Cross*. Minneapolis, MN: Fortress, 2004.

Thompson, Michael. *Where is the God of Justice? The Old Testament and Suffering*. Eugene, OR: Wipf and Stock, 2011.

Torrance, Thomas F. *The Mediation of Christ*. Edinburgh: T & T Clark, 1992.

Tacey, David. "Fragments: the Spiritual Situation of our Times." In *God, the Gift and Postmodernism*, edited by Caputo, John. and Michael Scanion, 170–184. Bloomington: Indiana University Press, 1999.

Bibliography

Underhill, Evelyn. *The Mystics of the Church*. New York: Schocken, 1964.

Upjohn, Sheila. *In Search of Julian of Norwich*. London: Darton, Longman and Todd, 1989.

Vanhoozer, Kenin. "The Atonement in Postmodernity." In *The Glory of the Atonement: Biblical, Theological & Practical Perspectives*. Edited by Charles E. Hill and Frank A. James III, 367-404. Downers Grove, IL: InterVarsity, 2004.

Vanier, Jean. *Drawn into the Mystery of Jesus through the Gospel of John*. London: Darton, Longman and Todd, 2004.

Vanstone, W.H. *The Stature of Waiting*. Darton, Longman and Todd, 1982.

Volf, Miroslav. *Exclusion and Embrace: A Theological Exploration of Identity, Otherness, and Reconciliation*. Nashville: Abingdon, 1996

———. *Free of Charge: Giving and Forgiving in a Culture Stripped of Grace*. Grand Rapids: Zondervan, 2005.

Waddel, Helen. *Peter Abelard*. London: Twentieth Century Classics, 1971.

Walters, Gwenfair M. "The Atonement in Medieval Theology." In *The Glory of the Atonement: Biblical, Theological & Practical Perspectives*. Edited by Charles E. Hill and Frank A. James III, 239-262. Downers Grove, IL: InterVarsity, 2004.

Ward, Keith. *Is Religion Dangerous?* Oxford: Lion, 2006.

———. *The Big Questions in Science and Religion*. West Conshohocken, PA: Templeton Foundation, 2008.

Watson, Philip. *Let God be God: An Interpretation of the Theology of Martin Luther*. London: Epworth, 1960.

Watson, Natalie. "A Wider View or the Place where Love is Possible: Feminist Theology, the Cross and the Christian Tradition." Unpublished Paper.

Weaver, Denny. "Response to Boersma." In *Atonement and Violence: A Theological Conversation*, edited by John Sanders, 73-79. Nashville: Abingdon, 2006.

Weingart, Richard. *The Logic of Divine Love: A Critical Analysis of the Soteriology of Peter Abelard*. Oxford: Clarendon, 1970.

Wendel, Francois. *Calvin: The Origins and Development of his Religious Thought*. Collins, 1965.

Whale, J. S. *The Protestant Tradition: An Essay in Interpretation*. Cambridge: Cambridge University Press, 1955.

———. *Victor and Victim: The Christian Doctrine of Redemption*. Cambridge: Cambridge University Press, 1960.

Williams, Rowan. *Open to Judgement: Sermons and Addresses*. London: Darton, Longman and Todd, 1994.

Wilson, A.N. *Dante in Love*. London: Atlantic, 2011.

Wright, N. T. *Jesus and the Victory of God*. Minneapolis: Fortress Press, 1996.

Winter, Michael. *The Atonement*. Problems in Theology. London: Chapman, 1995.

Wood, Ralph. *The Gospel according to Tolkien: Visions of the Kingdom in Middle-earth*. Louisville, KY: Westminster John Knox, 2003.

Young, Frances. *Sacrifice and the Death of Christ*. London: SPCK, 1975.